Moments in
Mathematics
Coaching

Moments in
Mathematics
Coaching

Improving
K–5 Instruction

Kristine Reed Woleck

CORWIN
A SAGE Company

For information:

Corwin
A SAGE Company
2455 Teller Road
Thousand Oaks, California 91320
(800) 233-9936
Fax: (800) 417-2466
www.corwin.com

SAGE Ltd.
1 Oliver's Yard
55 City Road
London EC1Y 1SP
United Kingdom

SAGE India Pvt. Ltd.
B 1/I 1 Mohan Cooperative
    Industrial Area
Mathura Road, New Delhi 110 044
India

SAGE Asia-Pacific Pte. Ltd.
33 Pekin Street #02-01
Far East Square
Singapore 048763

Printed in the United States of America

Library of Congress Cataloging-in-Publication Data

Woleck, Kristine Reed.
Moments in mathematics coaching: improving K–5 instruction/Kristine Reed Woleck.
    p. cm.
Includes bibliographical references and index.
ISBN 978-1-4129-6584-2 (pbk.)

    1. Mathematics—Study and teaching (Elementary) 2. Mathematics teachers—In-service training. I. Title.

QA135.6.W6 2010
372.7—dc22   2009038921

This book is printed on acid-free paper.

10   11   12   13   14   10   9   8   7   6   5   4   3   2   1

Acquisitions Editor:	Cathy Hernandez
Editorial Assistant:	Sarah Bartlett
Production Editor:	Jane Haenel
Copy Editor:	Tomara Kafka
Typesetter:	C&M Digitals (P) Ltd.
Proofreader:	Sarah Duffy
Indexer:	Terri Corry
Cover and Graphic Designer:	Anthony Paular

Contents

Preface

I remember with uncanny clarity my first year as a K–8 mathematics staff developer, responsible for the ongoing, job-embedded professional development of all K–8 mathematics teachers in a working-class public school district in New England. I was the only person in that position in the district, so I had to work hard to carve out my own professional development opportunities, find tools of reflection, and connect to others who were undertaking similar work with teachers. In many ways, I felt overwhelmed; at the same time, I felt invigorated and passionate about my work in a way I had never felt before.

I needed to define my role and work for myself. I chose the focus that felt not only most powerful but also (selfishly) of greatest interest to me. That is, I chose to focus on what was happening in mathematics classrooms across the district, recording student discussions about mathematics during those classroom visits, meeting with teachers to share what I heard their students saying, and discussing with teachers the implications for instruction and student learning. As I spoke with other professionals, I realized more and more that the work I was doing was coming to be known as "coaching" in the field of mathematics education. I had no guidebook, no road map for this coaching work; like so many others at the time and today, I was figuring it out as I went along.

Writing has always been a vehicle of reflection for me, and I soon found myself spending endless hours at night journaling about my experiences in my new position. The journal became a tool for my own professional development as a coach. Over time, I revisited my journal entries and reflected on them. What aspect of the coaching experience that I recorded did I struggle with the most? How did my work connect from one day to the next, from one teacher to the next? What themes were emerging in my work? I then shaped these journal entries into a set of coaching cases. I held onto those first cases and continued to write more with each year of coaching I undertook. Those cases and my journal writing became the seeds of this book.

The chapters of this book offer a variety of research connections, additional readings, templates to weave into practice, and other practical coaching tools that I have found effective, but each of the chapters is grounded in a coaching case from my journal over the past nine years in elementary math classrooms. These cases are not meant to serve as "recipes" for coaching; rather, they can allow all of us to "freeze" a moment of coaching, to unpack and examine that moment, and so discuss elements of the mathematics, student learning, and coaching moves and interactions that seem critical. Cases allow for this thoughtful, reflective examination of coaching so that we are then better able to make effective coaching decisions when doing the work in our respective schools and districts.

This book is intended to serve as a resource for those who support the mathematics professional development of teachers. This audience includes math coaches, math specialists, curriculum coordinators, staff developers, teacher leaders, and administrators. The book is grounded in mathematical content and experiences from the elementary level (K–5), but educators working in similar roles at the secondary level or in disciplines other than mathematics will also find the book useful as a professional text because the core elements of coaching that are developed here transcend levels and disciplines. University instructors will find this text relevant and powerful for use in programs and courses designed to support mathematics leaders and coaches in elementary schools.

The first section of this book presents an overview and broad images of the coach's work in elementary mathematics classrooms. Chapter 1 shares one snapshot of a coaching encounter in a classroom. This encounter and a review of coaching models that can be found in research and professional literature are used to articulate critical elements of coaching that will be revisited and examined in greater depth throughout the book. Chapter 2 discusses the behind-the-scenes organization and planning that can set the stage for successful entry into coaching with a group of teachers and help the coach get started. Chapter 3 describes a full coaching cycle, from the prelesson planning to the classroom visit to the postlesson debriefing meeting. Through the example presented in the case, strategies for navigating each segment of this standard coaching cycle are offered and highlighted.

The second section of this book then discusses tools for mathematics coaching; each chapter presents a specific tool and uses a case to illustrate and examine that tool. Chapter 4 discusses how curriculum resources themselves and the interaction between teacher, student, and curriculum can provide artifacts of practice that are valuable in coaching work. Chapter 5 addresses questioning as a tool for coaching; it describes several different types of questions that a coach may pose and the purpose of each. Chapter 6 notes the need at times to be explicit with a teacher in order to move practice forward. Chapter 7 discusses ways in which data can be harnessed both as a tool and leverage point for the coach's work with teachers.

The third section of the book presents coaching dilemmas, situations that may emerge and often prove challenging for the coach to navigate. In Chapter 8, situations are presented in which the coach must decide how to address teachers' classroom errors. Chapter 9 considers the role of demonstration or model lessons in the coach's work and how to ensure that such lessons are effective from the perspective of teacher professional growth. In Chapter 10, the point is made that the coach is a learner; how then does this reality conflict with staff notions of the coach as an "expert"?

The final section of this book calls attention to the need to provide professional development opportunities for the coach. Vehicles and structures to support the coach's growth are described in Chapter 11. Across all sections of the book, chapters conclude with focus questions that can serve as springboards for reflection and discussions with others. In all of the chapters, I strive to make my reflections on my work transparent, modeling the power of this reflective stance for continued growth.

Furthermore, a consistent structure of subheadings has been used for each case presented in a chapter to guide the reader. Each case is launched with the subheading Setting the Stage to introduce the context of the case—the grade level, relevant information regarding the teacher and coach relationship, etc. The case then begins to unfold in terms of the actions and dialogue in the classroom or between the coach and teacher. Lucy West and Fritz Staub (2003) refer to "coaching moves" in their work, and so the subheading Making the Move is used to note the moment of coach decision making in each case; this section of the case describes the decision-making process and the move that is made by the coach in the moment. Each case also includes a Taking a Closer Look discussion to analyze for the reader the decision-making process that was undertaken by the coach in the case, the pros and cons of the decision, and the relevant connections to research and models of coaching.

I am excited to share my coaching experiences and learning with a larger audience, but I am also cautious. I am sharing here the details, the struggles, and the successes of the work that I have undertaken with teachers and children over the past nine years across three different states. I would ask that readers respect the sensitive nature of the cases in this book and the courage of coach, teachers, and children as together they navigate the teaching and learning of mathematics.

I encourage you to use this book not merely as professional reading but as a tool for your own professional growth. Keep a journal close to you, jot down your thoughts and reflections, and share these with others. Use the tools that are provided and be explicit with others that you are studying all of this. That is how coaching will continue to evolve and grow for all of us.

Acknowledgments

I have been fortunate over my career to have worked with many remark-able mentors and colleagues in education, and each has influenced a dimension of who I am as a teacher, coach, and mathematics educator. To Marion Reynolds and Hal Melnick, thank you for opening my eyes and ears to young children's thinking.

I have also been fortunate to work in a school district that has afforded me the opportunity to grow professionally as a teacher leader. To my colleagues in the New Canaan Public Schools, thank you for embracing the challenges of coaching as together we foster young children's mathematical thinking.

I would like to extend special thanks to Dr. Mary Kolek, deputy super-intendent of the New Canaan Public Schools, for her vision, her intelli-gence and expertise, her affirmation, validation, and support of my work, and her inspiration.

I thank Cathy Hernandez, my editor at Corwin, for having the insight several years ago that mathematics coaching was important and encour-aging me to write about it; her patience, flexibility, and guidance encour-aged me to keep moving forward with chapters and drafts at those times when I wondered if anyone would ever want to read any of this.

And finally I thank my husband, Greg, and my daughter, Grace, for the time, patience, and unconditional love they have given to me along the way.

PUBLISHER'S ACKNOWLEDGMENTS

Corwin gratefully acknowledges the contributions of the following reviewers:

Lenisera Barnes-Bodison
Elementary Math
   Coordinator
DeKalb County School System
Decatur, GA

Susan Barrett
Federal Programs School
   Improvement Coordinator
Nicholas County Schools
Summersville, WV

Linda Bello
District Math Coach
Cranston School Department
Cranston, RI

Jamie Bolster-Beecham
Math Coach
Pendergast Elementary School
    District
Surprise, AZ

Cindy Bryant
Education Consultant,
    Mathematics
Missouri Department of
    Elementary and Secondary
    Education
Jefferson City, MO

Mollie S. Guion
Professional Learning Specialist
Austin ISD—PDC
Austin, TX

Euthecia Hancewicz
Mathematics Educator Support
    Services
Westhampton, MA

Loretta Heuer
Senior Research and Development
    Associate
Mathematics Learning and
    Teaching
Education Development Center
Newton, MA

Diane Kinch
Secondary Mathematics Specialist
Pomona Unified School District
Pomona, CA

Mary Kolek
Deputy Superintendent
New Canaan Public Schools
New Canaan, CT

Ellen Knudson
Mathematics
    Educational Consultant
Bismarck, ND

Alison Lee
Elementary Mathematics Expert
LAUSD, District 2
North Hollywood, CA

Dana R. Martin
Elementary Math Trainer
Southern Nevada Regional
    Professional Development
    Program
North Las Vegas, NV

Sharon Mueller
Math Content Coach, K–6
Center for Academic Excellence
St. Paul, MN

Judith Rogers
K–5 Mathematics Specialist
Tucson Unified School District
Tucson, AZ

Joan Salamanchuk
Math Coach
Housman Elementary School
Houston, TX

Ellen B. Scales
Assistant Professor of Education
Drexel University
Philadelphia, PA

About the Author

 **Kristine Reed Woleck** is the K–5 mathematics coordinator for the public schools in New Canaan, Connecticut. Prior to this position, she served as a K–8 staff developer, math coach-specialist, and mathematics consultant in both public and private schools in New York, Massachusetts, and Connecticut. She began her career as a first-grade teacher in Connecticut.

Kris's graduate studies in the Bank Street College of Education Mathematics Leadership Program sparked her interest in teacher leadership in mathematics and prompted her to pursue her study of staff development and ultimately coaching. With a sixth-year diploma in educational leadership and administration from the University of Connecticut, she is interested in examining how school administrators can most effectively bring principles of coaching into their supervision of teachers.

Kris has authored several articles in professional journals based on her classroom teaching experiences, coaching work, and her experience as a facilitator of online coaching seminars in conjunction with the Education Alliance at Brown University. Her work has been published in *Teaching Children Mathematics*, the 2001 *Yearbook of the National Council of Teachers of Mathematics*, and the *Journal of Staff Development*. Most recently, she was selected as a 2009–2010 Classroom Teaching Fellow in the U.S. Department of Education Teaching Ambassador Fellowship program to include practitioner perspectives and voice in the development of educational policy.

PART I

The Coach's Work

1

What Is Coaching?

Before moving into this opening chapter, consider the following questions for reflection:

- What is the role of a mathematics coach?
- How would you define coaching? What images come to mind?
- What renders coaching effective?

There are coaches in many professions. There are athletic coaches. There are business coaches. There are financial coaches. And now there are coaches in schools. Operationalizing a definition of coaching in schools, however, can be elusive. What does this coaching look like in practice? What does the coach do in a school or classroom? What does the teacher do when he or she is being coached? How do you know if coaching has been successful or effective?

This opening chapter presents a case intended to provide one example of a coaching encounter; by analyzing this interaction between a teacher and coach, essential elements of coaching will surface. Discussion will then turn to several research-based models of coaching that reflect these essential coaching elements. This sets a foundation for the chapters that follow in which cases unpack and illustrate essential elements of coaching and describe how various coaching dilemmas are navigated.

Case: Coaching in Action ∞ Ann, Grade 5

This case presents a fifth-grade classroom where students were engaged in a game activity to develop fluency with mental math subtraction strategies. My interactions with a student during this class session provided me with insights into the pitfalls some students were falling into in their subtraction work. In a private conference with the teacher "on the side," I was able to use the student observations as a vehicle to draw out further questions, connections, and self-reflection from the teacher. I was also surprised to learn that the teacher did not have a clear understanding of the mathematical purpose of the activity. All of this brought new insights to my coaching agenda for her.

SETTING THE STAGE

Ann's fifth graders worked in pairs playing "Close to 0," a game intended to develop fluency and flexibility with mental math broadly and subtraction strategies specifically (Kilman, Tierney, Russell, Murray, & Akers, 2004). The students were to arrange a set of digit cards in such a way as to create two three-digit numbers whose difference was as close to zero as possible. Both Ann and I circulated among the pairs to note our observations on Post-its.

Paul had arranged his digits in the following manner:

$$364$$
$$-353$$

He moved his finger down each column from right to left, subtracted each separately, and arrived at a difference of 11. He was quite satisfied with that arrangement. He had already demonstrated an ability to persist in this work in the earlier rounds of the game I had observed, so I decided to prompt him to think further about arrangements of the digits. I asked if there was another way to arrange the digits; he began to try moving some of the digits, but each time he placed the 3 above the 4, he would quickly move it back.

What was going on here? Was he avoiding this because, using his strategy of doing the traditional column subtraction, he would need to borrow mentally and hold that in his head? That seemed to be his only approach to subtraction. I wanted to push him to inspect the numbers as whole quantities and to consider strategies of counting up—of seeing the relationship between addition and subtraction and using landmark numbers. Now how could I push him to consider these other computational strategies? It was becoming evident to me how much I learn through this coaching work in classrooms—that is, how my own understanding of children's development of mathematical ideas (and how to support that development) grows as I listen to children and teachers in the classroom.

I decided to pose the possibility of 363 − 354 to him and see how he would tackle it. I moved the digits and then asked him, "How about this arrangement?" Paul thought for a moment and seemed to begin to apply his traditional borrowing technique. I commented on what I noticed him doing and asked, "Is it sometimes hard for you to keep all those numbers in your head?"

He looked relieved as I acknowledged his hard work and effort. "Yes!" he said.

I encouraged him to look at the numbers as a whole and reminded him that he may know some landmark numbers that could be useful here. We had already talked together in an earlier round about counting up as being another strategy when finding differences, so I referred to this as well.

Paul then announced, "So, 6 more would get me to 360, then plus 3. That's 9!"

This counting-up strategy using landmark numbers was an indication of Paul's number sense, and it certainly was carried out with greater ease than the mental borrowing he had been trying with those numbers.

MAKING THE MOVE

A few minutes later, Ann and I moved off to the side of the room together, accessible to the children but able to converse about our observations. I wanted to share my interaction with Paul, but I first wanted to hear Ann's interpretations of the children's work.

"What have you noticed?" I asked.

She described that her students would avoid arranging the digits in such a manner that a "bigger number in the ones place would need to be subtracted from a smaller number in the ones place." They would avoid this situation and so were not exploring arrangements of the digits that would lead to differences closer to zero. Ann attributed this to the fact that they were avoiding borrowing since they needed to do this mentally and did not have pencil and paper for the game. But, she said, she wasn't sure what to do about it.

I was able to confirm her observations by sharing excerpts from my notes about Paul with her. As I told Ann of my interactions with Paul, she indicated that this was what she had been seeing with others in the classroom and was glad to hear how I approached it with him.

"That's good for me to hear what you did because I'm not always sure if I should do anything or not or if I should show them something or not," Ann said.

This comment made me think that Ann was working hard to find a balance when supporting children's learning. This seemed like it would be important to talk more about with her. It seemed like an opportunity to explore the role of the teacher in math class.

But before I could say anything else, Ann came forth with another question: "So, what *is* the purpose of the game? I mean, I know it is in our program here, but I don't think in the three years I have been teaching it that I've really ever known what it's meant to do."

Her question took me by surprise. I realized then that I had overlooked this very important question. I had assumed that Ann recognized the purpose and mathematical objectives of the game and that she saw how this game was a tool for supporting computational fluency strategies, building on games and work the children had encountered while developing efficient strategies in other grades. But then it occurred to me that this game was coming in the midst of a unit in which Ann had seen the focus as factors, multiples, and strategies for multiplication and division. Ann had also not taught at any other grade level; most likely, she was not familiar with the work on addition and subtraction strategies that is done at other grades.

I felt speechless for a moment. Although I understood the mathematical goals of the game, I wondered how I should approach this question with Ann. How could I help her to make sense of the ideas herself right here and recognize the mathematical *agenda* that the game promoted? I decided to refer back to Paul, and we compared his two strategies again. This gave us a context for a discussion about developing fluency with addition and subtraction—fluency grounded in landmark numbers, number sense, and number relations.

"Then," Ann remarked, "when I see Sarah doing 303 – 298 on a piece of paper it *is* good for me to stop and ask her to think about how far away 298 is from 300 so she can do it in her head!" It felt like we were both making sense of our observations of children and determining ways to support their mathematical growth. Ann looked relieved to have had her instincts validated by our brief conversation as the students continued to work. "I've been teaching this for three years, but now I think I finally understand the purpose of this game," she exclaimed.

This made me realize that there are instances in which learning goals and purposes may be obvious to the authors of an instructional text or curriculum program but must be made more explicit for a teacher. This, then, must be a part of my work as a coach.

TAKING A CLOSER LOOK

This encounter with Ann serves to illustrate a broad collection of essential elements of coaching:

- A trusting teacher-coach relationship
- A focus on deepening mathematical content and pedagogical content knowledge
- The effective use of questioning techniques
- Listening skills
- Coaching discussions grounded in student thinking and student work

Not only are these elements of coaching evident in Ann's case, but they will emerge in a variety of other coaching encounters presented in the cases throughout this book.

Perhaps the most critical element of this coaching encounter with Ann was the teacher-coach relationship that had been built over our months of working together. It was the trust in that relationship that gave Ann permission to make public her own questions about curriculum content and her instructional practices in the classroom. With careful listening, I could gather insights to inform the direction not only of this particular coaching interaction but of future sessions with Ann that could deepen her mathematical and pedagogical content knowledge.

Launching the teacher-coach dialogue with an open-ended question such as "What have you noticed?" not only allowed me to move forward from Ann's level of understanding and focus, but it also communicated to Ann a spirit of collaboration and validated her own observations of the students. With such an open-ended question, the coaching encounter also ensured that Ann reflected on practice and student learning in the moment. What's more, the entire coaching encounter remained grounded in students' work and mathematical thinking, the shared interest of both teacher and coach. Paul's thinking in particular provided a neutral ground for discussing the issue impacting student learning.

RESEARCH-BASED MODELS OF COACHING

The essential elements of coaching illustrated in Ann's case are also the common threads that are found throughout coaching definitions and models presented in research and professional literature. Researcher Jim Knight (2006) defines coaching as "a nonevaluative, learning relationship between a professional developer and a teacher, both of whom share the expressed goal of learning together, thereby improving instruction and student achievement" (para. 6). Koh and Neuman (2006) reviewed research related to coaching with respect to literacy and compiled a set of 10 "exemplary elements of coaching." These exemplary elements include coaching that is on-site, ongoing, and sustained over time; coaching that aims to facilitate teacher reflection; coaching that provides descriptive feedback to teachers; and coaching that results in improved student outcomes.

There are a variety of models that can be considered, compared, and contrasted as we seek to bring greater clarity to coaching and develop coaching practices that remain true to the essential elements of coaching and best serve a given context and school community.

All of the models speak to the importance of establishing respectful and trusting relationships with teachers in coaching work. All of the models make the call, either implicitly or explicitly, for sufficient time for coaches to work with teachers. This is time that should be devoted to collaborative learning conversations that allow the coach to serve as a mediator of reflection, as the conduit from the lesson to the teacher's reflection and learning. All of the models also make the call for professional development for coaches, recognizing that coaches need to develop expertise not only in content knowledge related to mathematics and pedagogy but also coaching skills, questioning techniques, and other professional skills that allow them to best promote adult learning.

Yet there are differences as well. Some models, such as content-focused coaching, are specific to mathematics coaching, while others, such as cognitive coaching, are coaching models that cut across disciplines. The intent here is not to provide a full literature review of coaching research but rather to provide an overview of the models that may serve as valuable resources to a mathematics coach. In this overview, four models will be discussed: (1) Art Costa and Robert Garmston's Cognitive Coaching, (2) content-focused coaching described in the work of Lucy West and Fritz Staub, (3) Jim Knight's instructional coaching, and (4) the pedagogical content coaching model described by David Foster and used by coaches in the Silicon Valley Mathematics Initiative. Each model contributes to the decision making that is apparent throughout the cases in this book; these are models that I have drawn upon and adapted in my own coaching work.

Cognitive Coaching

Art Costa and Robert Garmston developed Cognitive Coaching as a supervisory or peer coaching model that supports others as they enhance their own cognitive processes, including reflection and problem solving. Cognitive Coaching "enables people to modify their capacity to modify themselves" (Center for Cognitive Coaching, 2009, para. 1). In such a model, emphasis is on bringing the person being coached, not the coach, to the point of evaluating what is effective or ineffective about his or her own practice.

The model is based on a set of assumptions related to the cognitive processes necessary in teaching and the capacity of an individual for reflection and growth. The role of the coach is one of a mediator, "one who figuratively stands between a person and his thinking to help him become more aware of what is going on inside his head" (Center for Cognitive Coaching, 2009, para. 3). In Sparks's (1990) interview with Robert Garmston on Cognitive Coaching, Garmston elaborates further, stating, "This is a process of self-motivated and self-directed learning and the job of the coach is to support the teacher in this natural journey. The coach does this by becoming another set of eyes for the teacher and a mediator of the teacher's processing of his or her own teaching experiences" (p. 13). Self-coaching emerges as the goal of Cognitive Coaching.

As in all of the models, trust and rapport between the teacher and coach are the foundation. In Cognitive Coaching, the model then unfolds in the components of a preconference, a lesson observation, and a postconference. Questioning techniques during both the pre- and postconferences are open-ended and probe for teacher perspective and reflection. Responses by the coach to the teacher's reflections and comments are nonjudgmental. Attention is given in the postconference to supporting the teacher in recalling the lesson for reflection and discussion, rather than the coach sharing back what was observed (Sparks, 1990).

My philosophy of coaching is grounded in the notion of a coach as a mediator of teacher reflection. For this reason, I was drawn to the Cognitive Coaching model. The notion of building teacher independence and a stance of self-reflection by coaching through open-ended questioning is evident in many of the cases in the chapters that follow. However, as I began coaching in mathematics classrooms, I realized that Cognitive Coaching alone was not sufficient for my work with all teachers. I needed to consider the particular challenges of coaching elementary classroom teachers who may have limited comfort levels with the content; many of these teachers have a need for deeper content knowledge and deeper understandings of how children develop these ideas in order to systematically reflect on their practices. As I encountered the realities of coaching, I began to push the boundaries of the Cognitive Coaching model. I found myself raising questions:

- What does coaching look like if the teacher first needs to learn the mathematics for herself?
- Is there a time when coaching moves need to be more explicit and direct?
- What does that look like?

Content-Focused Coaching

The content-focused coaching model described by Lucy West and Fritz Staub (2003) addresses some of these questions, and their text brings a focus on mathematics coaching specifically at the elementary level. As such, it was the most obvious resource for my work as a coach. Content-focused coaching is content specific. Like other coaching models, it is grounded in a cycle of prelesson conferences, lessons, and postlesson conferences. Unique to content-focused coaching, the coaching conversations with a teacher make use of specific conceptual tools to focus and guide the conversations in a manner that develops the teacher's pedagogical content knowledge. These tools include a framework for lesson design, a set of learning principles, and a set of core issues in mathematics lessons. West and Staub state:

> Content-focused coaching zeroes in on the daily tasks of planning, teaching, and reflecting on lessons by suggesting a framework and tools for addressing standards, curriculum, principles of learning, and lesson design and assessment. It does not prescribe particular methods or techniques of teaching. (p. 2)

Though specific instructional techniques are not prescribed, the frameworks for coaches to use in coaching conversations with teachers are detailed and focus on examining the mathematics of a lesson and the intended student learning.

The specific focus on mathematics was particularly valuable to me as I began to build images of what coaching conversations in mathematics might sound like given the need to develop content knowledge with teachers. At the same time, the realities of my own coaching context, including time constraints, brought me to a more reflective stance toward content-focused coaching. I began to raise questions and challenge certain dimensions of the model. I needed to develop more flexible models of coaching that still remained true to the essence and intent of content-focused coaching. I also began to encounter teachers struggling with the establishment of classroom culture and classroom management; in some cases, it was impossible to get at the mathematics of a lesson because of these distractions. I needed to consider how to adapt a model of coaching to support these teachers as well.

Instructional Coaching

In his instructional coaching model, Jim Knight (2004) defines an instructional coach as an on-site professional developer who collaborates with educators to identify and assist with implementation of proven teaching methods. The work the instructional coach undertakes entails processes that are purposely designed and carried out over a series of coaching sessions. Enrolling and identifying teachers involves communicating to them the intent of instructional coaching, gauging interest levels among staff, and establishing the critical mass of teachers poised for coaching. Explaining, modeling, observing, exploring, supporting, and reflecting are the vehicles through which the coach supports the teacher in putting given instructional methods into practice in the classroom.

Knight (2007) also gives specific attention to the professional skills that are required in coaching, most notably with regard to communication. He addresses strategies to support active listening skills and body language when meeting with teachers. Moreover, his work is filled with templates: observation forms, teacher meeting logs, and Are You Interested? forms for enrollment. These are templates that build an organizational structure around the work of the coach.

Knight's work pushed me to consider, question, and adapt for myself tools that support the logistics of coaching. From session to session with a teacher, my initial coaching work felt disjointed and seemed to focus on the parts with little sense of how this was all fitting into the whole of the school. Turning attention to the organizational elements allowed me to communicate more effectively with teachers, better organize my time, monitor my work, and provide more focused follow-up and feedback to teachers.

Pedagogical Content Coaching in Mathematics

David Foster, program director of mathematics for the Noyce Foundation, has presented several papers that articulate the principles and practices that guide the pedagogical content coaching model. This is a model that is utilized for mathematics coaching in the Silicon Valley Mathematics Initiative (SVMI), an extensive project to improve the teaching and learning of mathematics in California. Within the structure of preteaching conferences, in-class experiences, and postlesson conferences, the focus of pedagogical content coaching is on students' thinking, understandings, and work products (SVMI, 2007a). Coaches vary the roles they play from modeling to team teaching to leading; in this model, the work of the coach can entail in-classroom coaching as well as facilitation of mathematics professional development meetings for teachers or administrators.

The fundamentals of successful coaching in the pedagogical coaching model parallel those noted in the case of Ann earlier in this chapter:

- A trusting relationship between the coach and teacher
- Time for preparation and reflection
- Clearly defined roles, responsibilities, and expectations
- Effective listening skills
- Strategic questions that promote thinking
- Data collection and thoughtful feedback related to teacher and student behaviors

These fundamentals marry the *content* of content-focused coaching with the attention to communication strategies found in Knight's instructional model. In this way, the pedagogical content coaching model strikes a balance that calls for an emphasis on reflection but recognizes the multiple roles that a coach may play based on the needs of and relationships with the teacher.

KEYS TO DEVELOPING A COACHING MODEL

As described in this chapter, there are several models that can inform the work of a mathematics coach; a coach can choose any one of these models to study and emulate in practice. At the same time, coaching is situational work that is impacted by the constraints of a school's context. Learning communities are at different stages of development in different districts or schools, and a coach needs to take this into consideration when embarking on the work.

Mathematics curricula in one district may set a foundation for rich discussions of student work that the coach can build upon with teachers. In another district, a given math textbook may offer little springboard for conversations about student thinking. An administrator in one school may have spent the past two years establishing structures that provide teachers with time to meet as grade-level teams and with curriculum-based coaches, opening teachers' minds to the value of coaching sessions and reflection. In another school, teachers may have neither common planning time nor any experience with structures that support professional dialogue. Such a wide range of possible contexts makes it difficult to simply transplant a particular coaching model from one school or district to another.

But being aware of the essential or exemplary elements of coaching that must be present in order for coaching to be effective—elements that were noted in Ann's case and throughout the research cited in this chapter—allows a coach to make informed decisions about the work under any condition or context. Knowledge of these essential elements, coupled with knowledge of multiple coaching models, allows a coach to intentionally design an effective coaching model that best meets the needs of his or her specific context and circumstances. What's more, given the dynamic nature of learning environments for students and adults, it is likely that the model will need to be fluid and will continually evolve over time.

Questions for Reflecting and Linking to Practice

1. This chapter opened with the question: What is coaching? Revisit your initial response to that question after reading this chapter. What new perspectives or insights do you now have?

2. Now consider the question: What is coaching *not*?

3. What new questions have emerged for you from this opening chapter? Use these questions to frame and focus your reading of the chapters ahead.

2

Starting the School Year

In many districts, coaching is new and unchartered territory for those who are asked to work in these positions. Often classroom teachers move into mathematics coaching positions. They must then navigate the shift from a focus on teaching children to a focus on supporting children's learning indirectly through the growth of another teacher. There is no curriculum guide for coaching, no manual or map. In many cases, districts adopt coaching positions without clearly defined job descriptions; coaches are left to define their positions to meet the needs of the teachers and districts. Teachers themselves often have few images of the possibilities of working with a coach and as a result may be hesitant. This was the case for me as well, and I recall the overwhelming feelings that accompanied my first few months of coaching.

This chapter describes a variety of steps that other coaches and I have used to navigate the reality of implementing coaching in districts for which this model of professional development is new to both coaches and classroom teachers. The chapter will look at how a first-time coach begins to work with teachers (or how an experienced coach may enter into the work in a new school or district). Attention will be given to the importance of establishing trusting relationships with teachers as a coach, and we'll examine how the first coaching meetings with a teacher may be structured to support this building of trust. Finally, we'll consider the coach's relationship with the building administrator. What does this relationship look like and how can the coach shape it to best support the work being undertaken?

MAKING INTRODUCTIONS

Every September, I would welcome the first day of school with the thrill of getting to know a new group of children and establishing the classroom community and culture that would be ours for the next 10 months. But in my first year in a coaching position when the calendar turned to September, I found myself without a classroom of my own, and I found myself without the routines I knew so well. I wondered how to begin this work as a coach.

I planned to introduce myself and the new coaching position in the building at the back-to-school staff meeting. While this may have been my intended formal introduction, I quickly realized that many informal introductions happened as I encountered teachers in the copy room or around the building in late August when teachers returned to set up their classrooms. I made it a point to spend some days in late August setting up my own space in the school, and looking back on this, I see how beneficial those days were for the very purpose of meeting teachers.

I went to work unpacking boxes of manipulatives, student activity books, and other resources that teachers had requested for the school year, and I delivered these to their classrooms. This gave me the opportunity to become familiar with the layout of the building and the location of each teacher's classroom and name. More important, it was a very nonthreatening way to meet teachers. They were welcoming of anyone arriving with supplies for the classroom, and they were able to perceive me in a positive light as someone who was there to support them and someone who was competent in providing them with necessary materials.

Nevertheless, just before the first day of school, I did take the opportunity at the back-to-school staff meeting to formally introduce myself to the staff. I used that introduction to let teachers know something about my experience as a classroom teacher with children and something about who I am outside of "math." I mentioned my daughter, my husband, and my loyalty to the Red Sox—so important in that New England town. I wanted them to know my core values rest in children's learning, for this would be the common ground from which much of our work would build, but I also wanted them to see me as a whole person so they could enter into conversations with me early on in the hallways or in the staff room, even if mathematics felt intimidating to them.

For some teachers, coaching was not a familiar form of professional development and they needed to begin to understand how I might work with them. For that reason, I shared with the staff a brief overview of what coaching can be—from planning to coteaching to reflecting on student work together. I also used the introduction as an opportunity to let teachers know that their voices were important if we were to be sure that our work together would fit their needs; to do that, I needed to have time to talk with each of them and see their classrooms in action to understand the context of their practice.

This set the stage for me to share a calendar of open dates and times for meetings and classroom visits during the first month of school. I indicated to teachers that this calendar would be posted on the staff room door, and I asked that each of them sign up for a meeting either individually or as a grade-level team for us to talk further. All of this I had discussed previously with the building principal and grade-level team leaders to be certain of their support in moving forward with a schedule for these meetings and classroom visits. Some coaches post such a calendar or list of available meeting times electronically to facilitate sign-up for teachers, while others coordinate with administration to arrange coverage for teachers for these meetings so that prep or planning times need not be missed or resentment created. Whatever the format, what is important is that the expectation for these conversations is set. Then the coach's work can begin.

Taking the First Step

- Be visible

  Before the school year begins, in the copy room, in the teacher lunch room

- Lend a hand

  With materials, distributing resources

- Introduce yourself and your role at a staff meeting

  Give examples of what coaching work can be

- Post sign-ups and calendars for initial meetings

  With teams or individuals, arrange coverage for teachers if necessary

---

ESTABLISHING TRUST

A position paper presented by the SVMI (2007a) coaching project states, "Before any effective coaching can take place the coach and teacher must build a trusting relationship that promotes mutual respect and safety" (p. 2). This relationship building is not a single moment in time; it is an ongoing process that evolves to different levels over weeks, over months, even over years. In my experience, there are initial stages of establishing relationships with teachers as a coach that are about building credibility and getting to know the myriad of personalities in a school. There are stages that are built later when pushing a teacher to reflect on student work or practice. There are still deeper levels of the relationship that must be in place for the teacher to be a risk taker in the presence of a coach.

I knew the focus of my first year as a coach needed to be on getting to know the teachers and establishing the initial levels of trust with them. For that reason, as I met with each teacher or grade-level team during the first month of school, I used the meetings as a time to pose broad questions and listen to teachers' perspectives with regard to the district mathematics curriculum, student learning, and their own professional development interests and needs. Figure 2.1 presents one set of questions that may be used in such an initial coach meeting with a teacher.

Listening in a nonjudgmental manner was crucial in terms of letting teachers know that I was genuinely interested in a dialogue that involved sharing and considering different perspectives and challenging thinking. If I jumped to respond to a teacher's comment too quickly or in a tone that was perceived as overly defensive, it would quickly be thought that asking for the teacher's voice was more an exercise and not particularly respected. I nodded often. I paraphrased comments to let teachers know they had been heard and to ensure I understood their points and intentions. I sat beside teachers, not across from them; even body language and position communicates messages about the type of relationship a coach hopes to establish with a teacher.

In the staff room, in the copy room, and in the lunch room, I also talked to teachers. Sometimes the conversations were about materials teachers needed for math class or questions about unit sequence or pacing as teachers began their year; more often, the conversations were informal and had nothing to do with math. I visited classrooms as well. In those classroom visits, I joined in calendar routines. I worked with small groups during math choice time. I picked up what seemed like hundreds of colored beads that fell out of a bag during the cleanup of a patterns lesson in one kindergarten classroom. None of this was coaching per se. But all of it would render coaching possible in the future. Before I could get at the math, teachers needed to see me as a colleague they could trust, and I needed to build credibility in their eyes. Before I could coach a teacher and make decisions about the types of coaching moves or probing questions that might best fit that teacher, I first needed to understand that teacher's classroom and the young mathematicians at work there. There were times when all of this felt painfully slow.

DECIDING WHO TO COACH

Most of these conversations with teachers and initial visits to classrooms were smooth, ripe for developing relationships that could lead us into productive pieces of coaching work. There were some, however, that were more challenging. I recall one moment when I entered a fourth-grade teacher's classroom for our first meeting in the fall. She looked at me, and before I could even open the conversation with a greeting, she said, "I

Figure 2.1   Initial Coach Meeting Question Template

INITIAL COACH MEETING: *GETTING TO KNOW YOU*

Teacher: _____   **Date:** _____

School: _____   **Grade:** _____

Tell me about yourself.

What strengths do you see in the district's current mathematics program?

What questions or areas of concern do you have?

What goals do you have for yourself as a math teacher this year?

How do you learn best?

Is there anything else you'd like me to know?

---

don't know what your agenda is, but, look, I've been teaching longer than you've been alive." Needless to say, as a young, energetic, first-year coach expecting all teachers to be eager to work with me, I was speechless. I realized all I could do was to acknowledge she was correct in her statement and validate the more than 30 years of teaching experience she had. Sometimes that is all you can do.

There were other teachers who were more subtle in their messages. For instance, there were those who simply would not sign up for an initial "getting to know you" meeting. There were those who would meet me at the door when I arrived with supplies, and then with a smile and a thank you, they would politely close the door with no invitation to enter the classroom. One teacher even locked the classroom door so that I could not come in during the lesson.

In my first year as a coach, I spent much time and energy thinking about how I could push these teachers to open their classroom doors to me, how I could work with them as a coach. But when I considered all of the other teachers in the building, I realized that as a coach, I needed to prioritize who it was that I would coach. Coaching is demanding work, with a significant time commitment not only for classroom visits but also for planning and debriefing-reflection sessions. It is an intense time commitment not only for the teacher but for the coach, and so it becomes critical that the coach has purposely and carefully selected those teachers with whom to work for a given period of the school year.

An important factor to consider in this selection of teachers for coaching is the developmental level of the teacher; there is variability among teachers in terms of readiness to engage in the work with a coach. Teacher development can be described from multiple perspectives, but what has been most critical in my experience is the openness to new learning, collaboration, and reflection demonstrated by the teacher. Often the teachers who fit this description are either novice teachers (in their first three to four years in education) or veteran teachers who are out "ahead of the pack" in terms of their practice, constantly searching for the latest research or seminar. There are arguments that can be made for and against beginning your coaching work with either of these two groups.

In the case of nontenured teachers, there is the argument that these teachers may be working intently to settle into their own teaching style and may find the level of work with a coach to be a mismatch for their level of concerns in the classroom. To raise another view, these new teachers are often the staff members who are most open to professional support and learning and so may be most willing to give up a prep or lunch period or time before or after school to meet with a coach. With these teachers, the coach should be prepared to focus initially on elements of effective classroom structures and the building of classroom culture that supports deep learning of mathematics. In some cases, coaches may encourage first- and second-year teachers to work closely with their mentor teachers in the building in order to establish their classroom communities and management approaches.

Some coaches feel that teachers in their third and fourth year of teaching may be more appropriate for coaching in that their concerns level will have moved beyond immediate concerns of the daily routines and classroom management and are now available to delve deeper into curriculum and instructional practices to better address diverse student needs in their classrooms. Other coaches feel that working with first- and second-year teachers is critical because it allows a coach to ensure that these teachers are developing a robust, reflective lens for mathematics teaching and learning from their first years in classrooms. Regardless of the exact timing, coaching of early-career teachers speaks to the building of capacity and sustainability in the school with an eye toward the future.

In the case of veteran teachers who are filled with an eagerness to learn and develop their practice still further, there are some (i.e., coaches and administrators) who may feel that these are not the most "needy" of the teachers and so question if it is the most effective use of a coach's limited time. Such a perspective needs to be reframed in the context of building math leaders in the school and satisfying the professional learning needs of our most competent teachers. When competent veteran members of a faculty work with a coach and grow still further in their own practice, the spheres of mathematics leadership can expand and these veteran teachers can emerge as teacher leaders that will allow the influence of the coach to spread well beyond the direct work of the coach.

DECIDING WHO NOT TO COACH . . . THEN WHAT?

But what about those teachers who resist, either actively or passively? Aside from giving herself "permission" to focus on others in the building, what can the coach do to build productive relationships with these teachers and perhaps impact the teaching and learning of mathematics in those classrooms from afar? One answer rests in considering those vehicles of professional development aside from direct coaching that might be harnessed with these teachers. In some districts, coaches are hired specifically to work one-on-one with teachers, but in many other districts, the coaching role is embedded in a larger position of staff developer, mathematics specialist, or mathematics coordinator. In these larger roles, the coach may also facilitate team meetings (grade level or cross grade) or study groups; when these meetings with teams of teachers in the building have already been built into the structure of the school day, they provide a forum for the coach to engage all teachers—even those who are resistant—in text-based discussions, video study of mathematics lessons, and opportunities to examine student work.

In these group meetings, those who are resistant may find the setting safer in terms of opening their minds to new ideas. They will certainly raise the hard questions and challenge all that is being discussed, but in doing so, they prompt all of us to reaffirm our commitment and push us to keep a close eye on the student learning that supports our work. As the coach allows and even invites these hard questions to be raised and discusses them in a respectful manner, the coach gains credibility. As colleagues share the growth they are seeing in their own practice and student learning as a result of their coaching experiences, those who are resistant may also begin to slowly "have a go" with new ideas in their own classrooms and ultimately open their doors to a coach. It takes time, but these other group forums for professional dialogue and discourse play a role in planting the seeds for future coaching work.

This raises the point that the coach needs to keep in mind a long-term learning agenda that includes *all* teachers—novice and veteran, eager and resistant. This may be a learning agenda that is varied and develops across multiple years to bring all teachers into the work, but it must pay attention to all teachers in some intentional and strategic way. Why? Because there is an equity issue at hand here. That is, *all* students—not just those of teachers who are willing to work with a coach—deserve access to teachers who develop, reflect upon, and refine their instructional practice in an ongoing basis with the guidance and expertise of a coach.

There are occasions in which a building principal or district-level administrator may approach a coach to request that coaching be provided to a struggling teacher as part of a structured assistance plan. This is an awkward position for the coach, for it begs the conversation with the administrator about the importance of trust and willingness to engage in coaching that factors heavily into the success of the teacher-coach relationship. If the urgency of the situation brings the teacher to a point of willingness, it can serve as an entry point for the coach to work with a teacher who perhaps previously was resistant or ambivalent to the coach. But if the teacher is resistant to the coach's support, this needs to be brought forward to the administrator promptly in order to develop a plan in which the administrator works with the teacher to shape the urgency of the situation before moving to the coaching component.

In all cases, the coaching work is intended to support teacher growth and development, not serve as formal evaluation. The coach can share with an administrator the objective details of the level of support offered (e.g., list of meeting dates, classroom observations, and model lessons), but in no instance should the coach provide evaluative comments to the administrator unless explicit consent has been given by the teacher. This would erode the trust and confidentiality embedded in the work of coaching. We will discuss these boundaries of the coach's work a bit later in this chapter.

GETTING ORGANIZED

After my rounds of meeting with individual teachers and teams of teachers to assess their openness and readiness for coaching work, I had a core group of teachers who had made known to me verbally, via e-mail, or with a simple note in my mailbox that they were interested in establishing a time to work with me. Some coaches present teachers with a ready-made RSVP sheet when meeting with them individually or in small groups, and this sheet provides the teacher with a vehicle for expressing interest in working with a coach further. Given the busy lives of teachers, particularly at the beginning of a school year, such a simple slip of paper helps some teachers take the initiative to make known their interest in working with a coach.

As I began setting up planning sessions with teachers and classroom visits, I realized that I needed some sort of system to organize and log my work. Otherwise, despite all the best intentions, specific details of my conversations with teachers would fade from memory over time and my work with teachers would remain primarily in the moment, as that would be what was freshest in my mind. Given the ongoing nature of coaching, it is critical not merely to remain in the present but to also be able to look back where the work has evolved from and to have in mind an overarching plan or vision that guides your next steps with a teacher. That requires documentation.

I decided that a lined notepad and a clipboard could serve my purposes well. I could jot down my notes on the pad and flip easily to past notes. I could jot down questions to frame our discussions ahead of time. I could slip a sheet of guiding questions or an observation guide onto the clipboard; I could also keep multiple copies of handouts that I found useful to share with teachers on the clipboard to have them readily at hand. On the clipboard, I taped a copy of my monthly schedule (current and next month) in order to easily schedule the next coaching visit with a teacher as we concluded our session.

I also kept a separate file folder for each teacher I worked with. After a coaching session, I could tear off the page or pages of notes and place them in the teacher's folder back in my office. In that folder, I also logged my time and the emphases of the coaching work for the given session on a coaching log sheet for that teacher (Figures 2.2 and 2.3). To some, this step of transferring from the notes on the notepad and clipboard to the file folder and logging in a coaching log may seem like an inefficient use of time. However, what I found was that taking this time meant I was also taking the time to reflect on the coaching session I had had with that teacher in the context of our ongoing work together. I could easily look back in the file to ensure follow-through and consistent support of the teacher from one coaching session to the next.

Figure 2.2   Coaching Log Template

Teacher: _____   _____

School: _____   Grade: _____

Professional Learning Goal/Focus:

_____

Date	Session	Focus	Follow-Up/Next Steps

Figure 2.3   Coaching Log: Tony

Teacher: Tony Galgone

School: North Elementary   **Grade:** 3

Professional Learning Goal/Focus: Establish mathematics workshop model as structure to support differentiation and guided math groups; deepen understanding of math content in curriculum

Date	Session	Focus	Follow-Up/Next Steps
September 10	Planning meeting	Considering room arrangement, materials, space for math workshop organization. Discuss math menu as a tool.	Tony to draft math menu for Week 1 of multiplication unit and organize materials/label work spaces in classroom, coteach to support launch on 9/17.
September 17	Coteaching	Launch math menu—model explicit language used to establish routines.	Tony to use lesson launch with focus on math menu routine for next three days; follow-up coach observation on 9/24.
September 24	Observation/debrief meeting	Effective structure in place for math workshop—launch, menu options, debrief. Importance of modeling language "groups of" when discussing multiplication (in context of problems about things that come in groups).	Shift next planning meeting focus from structure of math workshop to unpacking the mathematical focus of the lesson (so clear on math focus). Next meeting is planning meeting on 10/1.

I share this organizational system with you because it was one that worked for me. Others find that they prefer to travel with a pocket folder of coaching log sheets to use at each coaching session. Others keep a spiral coaching notebook as an ongoing journal of their coaching sessions. I know of coaches who have a three-ring binder that holds their plan book-scheduler, loose leaf paper for notes, and copies of templates or handouts that they feel might be useful in their coaching meetings with teachers. I imagine that in this age of technology, coaches will find new and efficient ways to use handheld devices and tablet PCs as organizing tools for their work as well.

The specific system you establish is completely at your discretion. What is important is that you do establish some sort of system for yourself in order to be able to keep perspective on the work you are doing. All too often, the slow nature of change can blind us to the progress that has been made; when you have documentation and artifacts to look back on, the growth becomes more evident. This can be critical in a climate of accountability and tight budgets when coaching positions may need to be justified and validated through evidence of impact. Conversely, you can also recognize when a teacher's growth seems to have become static and may call for a change in approach. Whatever system you establish for yourself, keep in mind that it is only when you are in the midst of the year that you will actually know for certain if it is a system that is working well. Be open to revising and refining it as the year goes on and from one year to the next.

COMMUNICATING WITH ADMINISTRATORS

There is a piece of "getting started" that I overlooked in my very first year as a coach. I focused in that first year as a coach on the conversations to have with teachers to build relationships and establish trust. It did not occur to me that conversations with building administrators were important foundational elements as well. The discussion here will focus on the school-based coach and the conversations such a coach would have with building administrators. It is important to note, however, that for a districtwide mathematics coach, these same conversations would need to be had with district administrators and with building administrators across the district as a collective group.

Just as the role of a coach may be new to teachers, coaching may also be new to the administrator. In some cases, a principal knowledgeable about coaching may have been instrumental in establishing the urgency, budget lines, and staff structures to bring a coach position into the school. In other cases, coaching positions may be brought into schools as part of a larger district initiative and principals themselves may be unfamiliar with what the coach's role is intended to be. In some cases, coaching positions may emerge in a school or district with no formal job description to reference or the role may evolve from an existing position. It becomes important then to have communication with the principal to discuss and clearly define the role and responsibilities of the coach in the building. This is critical to ensure from the beginning a shared understanding of the work the coach will undertake.

It is essential that administrators understand that the primary role of the coach is not one of remedial math tutor for struggling students or an enrichment teacher to high-performing students. There are other boundaries as well that are critical to establish if a coach is to truly have the time to work effectively with teachers. For instance, coaches should not be used as substitute teachers or lunch and recess aides. Certainly, emergency situations may arise in a school and in the spirit of collaboration, all staff may step up to supervise students or take on an extra duty, but if these supervisory assignments become the norm for the coach, then the work of supporting student learning through the professional growth of teachers cannot occur. It is most helpful to draft a clear, well-articulated statement of the coach's responsibilities (and the boundaries of this work) if no such statement exists in the district. Models for such guidelines regarding the duties and responsibilities of mathematics coaches are available in such resources as the Massachusetts Department of Education (2007) *Characteristics of Standards-Based Mathematics Coaching* document and the SVMI (2007b) *Philosophy and Overview* document.

With the role of the coach well defined, conversations with administrators should then turn to the issue of confidentiality. That is, if trusting relationships are to be built with teachers, administrators must understand that coaching conversations with teachers, scripts recorded while in classrooms, and other coaching artifacts are confidential, only to be shared with consent from the teacher. It is important to clearly separate the work of the coach from evaluation, both in the minds of the teachers and in the minds of the administrators. For this reason, many districts hire coaches under a teacher contract—not under an administrator contract—as a clear message that formal evaluation duties are not within the scope of the coach's work.

At the same time, coaches should establish with administrators a feedback loop that includes regularly scheduled meetings; these meetings should occur at least once each month and a schedule set at the beginning of the year (i.e., the first Thursday morning of every month) is often the best way to ensure the time is carved out. These meetings allow the coach to share with the building administrator general perspectives on professional growth in the building, leverage points for this growth, and obstacles that may be inhibiting the work. These meetings keep math on the administrator's "radar" screen and allow the administrator to be an ally the coach can turn to when issues of school culture, schedules, or budget impede the coaching work.

Such communication with administrators and coaches should also include conversations that support a shared vision of effective mathematics teaching and learning in classrooms. Conversations about the elements of effective practice that a coach is working to develop with staff must be shared explicitly with the principals and assistant principals, and progress (or lack thereof) related to these goals should be updated at each monthly meeting with administrators. This requires mathematics professional development tailored to the needs of the administrator to develop an eye for what to look for in the mathematics classroom. This may be undertaken through the dialogue at monthly meetings with building administrators (sharing examples of lessons from the curriculum, student work samples, coaching questions posed to teachers, etc.). Collaborative learning walks or classroom walkthroughs by administrators and coaches can be followed by time to debrief what was observed. Also, there are tools such as the Lenses on Learning courses and materials from the Education Development Center (http://www2.edc.org/CDT/cdt/cdt_admin.html) that provide a more formal seminar structure for a group of administrators to develop this understanding. When this mathematical eye has been sharpened for the administrators, they are better able to provide feedback and teacher assistance in the context of the evaluation cycle that aligns with and supports the coaching work in the building. What emerges then is a coherent, consistent support system for teachers.

KEYS TO GETTING STARTED

The sense of excitement, enthusiasm, and passion that we feel for this work as coaches can ignite all of us to want to jump in headfirst and hit the ground running as the school year opens. It is not always easy to hold back, but a more measured approach—with a clear vision of where you are going—allows you to build the foundation and the bridges that are invaluable to sustaining your work with teachers and impact growth in the long term. Framing your early work as a coach around the following action steps can allow you to do this. Sometimes you need to go slow to go fast.

Getting Started: The Coach's "To Do" List

- **Be visible.** The more teachers see you (in the copy room, delivering materials, at staff meetings), the more opportunities there are for making introductions, clarifying the role of the math coach, and becoming a known resource in the school.

- **Build relationships.** Begin with teacher conversations and meetings in which you listen carefully and intently to teachers as they share their concerns, needs, goals, and learning styles.
- **Get organized.** Developing a system of note-taking and logs for coaching sessions allows you to notice patterns in the work and monitor fidelity and consistency with teachers.
- **Decide "who."** By prioritizing who will work with a coach, an overall agenda for learning for teachers can be created. This can ensure targeted, intentional planning for each teacher in your coaching work. To ensure equity from the perspective of student learning, this also entails considering the other vehicles for professional growth that you will harness with those teachers who are resistant or not yet the focus of a coaching cycle.
- **Connect with the administrator.** Conversations with the administrator should be ongoing, scheduled, and consistent. These are conversations initially to define the coaching role and discuss confidentiality, but they then should shift to conversations that provide broad feedback regarding mathematics in the school, develop a shared understanding of effective practice, and note ways that an administrator can support the work of the coach.

Questions for Reflecting and Linking to Practice

1. Consider the understanding of coaching that exists in your school. How would you go about communicating and clarifying the role of the math coach to staff members?

2. Draft a set of initial coach meeting questions that you might use at the opening of the school year with staff members. Use the template in this chapter as a beginning draft if that is helpful. What questions would remain the same every year and what questions would be different as your work with a teacher grows from year to year?

3. Based on how the role of math coach (or coach in other curriculum areas) has been defined in your school or district, what explicit conversations are important for you to have with your building administrator at the beginning of the year to ensure shared understanding of the coach's role and work?

3

The Coaching Cycle

Much of the literature related to mathematics coaching presents a typical coaching cycle as one that consists of three components: a prelesson conference, a classroom lesson experience, and a postlesson conference (SVMI, 2007a; West & Staub, 2003). Within each component of this cycle there is significant work for the coach and teacher to take on together and many moments of decision making for the coach. What is the focus for the prelesson conference? What are the roles that a coach might take on in the classroom as the lesson is implemented? How is the postconference approached?

In the pages that follow, a coaching case is presented in the three segments of this typical coaching cycle—prelesson conference (or planning meeting), lesson, and postlesson conference (or debrief meeting). Commentary and discussion about each segment provide insights into this formal cycle within which moments of coaching and decision making occur. The intent is not to provide a formula for coaching, but rather to develop a framework of critical elements to consider when designing coaching sessions with teachers.

Case: Decision Making in the Coaching Cycle ∞ Fiona, Kindergarten

This case traces the series of prelesson, in-class, and postlesson conversations I had in a coaching cycle with a first-year kindergarten teacher. Throughout the coaching cycle, I found myself in the position of making decisions about (1) the mathematical focus to pursue; (2) how my role before, during, and after the lesson could best foster this teacher's growth; and (3) the probing questions I would pose to the teacher along the way.

SETTING THE STAGE

As part of new-teacher support in our district, I met each week with Fiona throughout the fall months in a scheduled mathematics coaching cycle. Typically, we met on Tuesday afternoons to discuss an upcoming lesson for the week. We would plan the lesson together in the context of the unit as a whole, and I would schedule to be in her classroom during the lesson. We would then meet either during her specials time on the afternoon of the lesson or the next day to reflect and debrief.

We were heading into the middle of October, and Fiona was ready to begin a unit about patterns with her kindergarteners. In the first lesson, children would construct snap cube trains made of eight cubes; they would then sort their trains as a class to determine those that were patterns and those that were not. This experience was intended to support children in developing their understanding of the meaning of what constitutes a pattern in mathematics.

THE PLANNING MEETING

I decided that in the prelesson conference, or planning meeting, I would focus our coaching conversation on the closing segment of the lesson in which each child brings one of the snap cube trains to the rug for sorting. These class discussions are critical lesson components that allow children to synthesize and reflect on their learning, but they can be the most challenging segments of lessons for teachers. Teachers often are not certain how to focus the discussion to bring out the mathematical goals of the lesson. It was particularly important in this kindergarten lesson that the discussion be structured to foster children's understanding of patterns, not merely a show-and-tell of their cube trains. For this reason, I wanted to be sure that Fiona thought through this part of the lesson during our time together. Below is an excerpt from our conversation.

KRW: As the children are working, they'll probably make a lot of different eight-cube trains. What kinds of trains do you want them to bring to the rug for the group discussion?

Fiona: I bet some of them will just make random arrangements. But I think there will be some AB patterns too, since that is what they'll see in the launch.

KRW: OK, and certainly we'll want some of those. Are there any other types of patterns you want to look for?

Fiona: Well, if someone made a pattern like blue, red, red, blue, red, red, would I want to have that one come to the rug, or is that just going to confuse everyone?

KRW:	Do you mean because it is not an AB pattern?
Fiona:	Right.
KRW:	What do you think?
Fiona:	I think some of them might think it's a pattern but some of them might not.
KRW:	And if you think about the goal of this lesson, it's for children to deepen their understanding of what makes a pattern be a pattern.
Fiona:	Then I should show that other one even though it's different than AB?
KRW:	I'd say yes. They need to see lots of examples of different patterns. The AB pattern is probably the most familiar to these children from what they've seen in preschool. They might even think that it's the only kind of pattern. But you want to stretch them further here, maybe even with an ABC pattern train eventually too since it has three colors, not just two like the others.
Fiona:	OK, so I'll look for all of those.
KRW:	Now, do you anticipate you'll have any children who are really going to have difficulty with this lesson?
Fiona:	Jonah will. He still doesn't count past four. Making a train of eight cubes is going to be so hard for him. And that's not even thinking about patterns yet!
KRW:	Hmm. What do you think might be a good support so he can be part of the lesson?
Fiona:	I don't know . . . (pause). Maybe if I give him the train that I use in the launch and tell him that his train needs to be the same size.
KRW:	So that would help him have a train that has eight cubes to bring to the discussion. What do you think he'll do in terms of pattern work?
Fiona:	He might copy the pattern on mine, or he might just put random colors together.
KRW:	I think either way would actually be fine for this lesson because it is the discussion at the end that really highlights what a pattern is. That's the work for everyone. So your goal is to get him to a place where he can be a part of that discussion by first having a train to sort in the mix with the others.

TAKING A CLOSER LOOK

By focusing our planning meeting on the discussion segment of the lesson, I was able to bring to the forefront the mathematics of the lesson—the different types of patterns that kindergarteners need to encounter as they begin to form understandings of patterns. I was able to do this in the context of student thinking and learning, raising thoughts about the misconceptions students might bring to the work and probing for reflection about the challenges some students might encounter. This allowed for conversation to be woven throughout the planning meeting about the ways that the instructional decisions of the teacher during the lesson might support the development of the mathematics goals both for the class and for individual students such as Jonah.

In this way, the conversation addressed the three critical elements of a coach's prelesson conference or planning meeting with a teacher: (1) the mathematics, (2) student learning, and (3) the pedagogy (implications for the lesson and instruction). Time constraints often necessitate emphasis on one element more than another, but as was evident in this example with Fiona, it is possible to weave in and out of these elements during the conversation through probing questions. Possible questions related to each of these three areas for a planning meeting are offered in Figure 3.1.

There are a variety of ways to approach each of these elements of the planning meeting. For instance, I often address the mathematics of a lesson by asking a teacher to do the math of the lesson with me in our planning meeting. In the case of a Grade 5 teacher preparing a multiplication lesson, she and I might each solve several multiplication problems from the lesson and discuss our strategies and approaches with each other, thereby opening dialogue about the potential approaches or pitfalls that might be demonstrated by the students at work on those same problems. Also, the planning meeting might include examining student work with regard to the level of student thinking in the classroom and potential next steps for students in an upcoming lesson. What remains essential is that the planning meeting pushes the teacher to have clarity about the mathematical focus of the lesson and the manner in which the lesson will be responsive to students. From there, the conversation can move to define the role of the coach and the role of the teacher during the classroom lesson. Let's turn attention to that piece of the coach's work next.

DEFINING THE FOCUS

Often, I will ask a teacher during a planning meeting to indicate what he or she is working on in terms of a professional learning goal. This puts forth the assumption that the teacher is viewing this coaching work not merely as an opportunity to have assistance in the classroom but as a professional learning opportunity that is focused on his or her own growth as

Figure 3.1   The Planning Meeting: A Coach's Guide

Below are three critical elements to guide a planning meeting between coach and teacher; sample questions that a coach may pose to a teacher are listed for each element. The coach should aim to structure the meeting to move from the mathematics to the students to the pedagogy; planning in this way will be new to many teachers (and some teachers may resist it), but it is critical in terms of deepening the mathematical and pedagogical content knowledge of the teacher and avoiding activity for activity's sake with no larger mathematical agenda.

1. **The mathematics:** Doing the math
   - What is the math? (Discussing the mathematical goals of the lesson)
   - What are the multiple ways of solving this task or problem?

2. **The students:** Looking at student work, considering student thinking
   - What prior knowledge or prior experiences are students bringing to this lesson?
   - How might students approach this new idea or new task?
   - What potential misconceptions might we see in student thinking?
   - Who do you anticipate will have difficulty in the lesson?
   - Who do you anticipate may need to examine these ideas at a deeper level?

3. **The pedagogy:** Considering the implications for instruction
   - What part of the lesson will be most challenging for students?
   - What structures or scaffolds might be useful either for the whole class or for a small group of struggling students?
   - What representations might provide powerful visual models for students?
   - What grouping strategies are you planning to use for each segment of the lesson?
   - How can some students be stretched to deeper levels of understanding?

These are provided not as a laundry list of questions to be exhausted at each planning meeting with a teacher but as a resource of potential emphases or focal points for a coach to consider when planning a prelesson conversation with a teacher or when in the midst of such a meeting.

---

a teacher of mathematics. It sends the message that the teacher must be an active learner in this work and it also allows the teacher to have shared ownership of the experience by defining the piece of learning that would be most valuable.

There are many different aspects of professional learning that the coaching experience might focus on, and in some cases in which a teacher is new to coaching, the coach may need to suggest a possible focus. The coach may want to consider the following when suggesting a possible focus:

- Is the teacher trying to grow in the use of higher-level questions?
- Is the teacher struggling to put into place a structure in the classroom that will support guided math groups and independent learners?

- Is the teacher interested in refining how she or he uses formative assessments in the classroom or how to use data to inform small groups?
- Is there a particular concept that students have been struggling to understand and that must be approached in a different manner?
- Are there particular students that the teacher is unsure how to support in math class?

COACH'S ROLE, TEACHER'S ROLE

These possible professional development emphases in turn suggest different roles for the coach and teacher during the classroom lesson. For instance, if the teacher is unsure how to facilitate a strategy discussion that is at the level of strategy comparison and analysis (rather than just a show-and-tell of strategies), the coach may model the questioning and facilitation moves at that point of the lesson for the teacher. The teacher would take on the role of observer, sitting alongside the coach, scripting the questions and facilitation moves as well as the student responses, so that together the coach and teacher can reflect on that segment of the lesson in the postconference. This ensures that the teacher is an active learner as the coach models the questioning and facilitation techniques. If a teacher has been working to develop his or her own use of higher-level questioning in the classroom, the coach may take on the role of observer and script the questions that the teacher poses during the math class; the coach and teacher would then analyze the level of questioning evident in the lesson script during the debriefing meeting. If a teacher is working to limit "teacher talk" time and maximize student work time during math class, the coach might observe and record the teacher talk in the lesson, while specifically noting the start time of each segment and transition of the lesson.

With so many possible roles for the coach and teacher during a classroom lesson, it is important that the roles be determined and defined for the lesson in the planning meeting. This prevents confusion as to who may be facilitating various segments of the lesson and also ensures that the coach does not enter a situation in which it is assumed that she or he has prepared a lesson to teach while the teacher attends to other work or classroom tasks. It ensures purposeful roles that support the teacher's growth and, indirectly, the students' learning, and it leads to shared ownership of the implementation of the lesson. This is shared ownership even if the coach or teacher is taking on the role of observer, because the focus for the observation has been jointly defined.

Part of defining the roles at the end of the planning meeting is establishing any explicit boundaries that are necessary. That is, if this is still early in the coaching work between the coach and teacher, and particularly if trust between the teacher and coach is still in its early stages of development, it is important to discuss such parameters as to how comfortable the teacher is with the coach interjecting during the lesson or how the coach will be introduced to the students. In this case with Fiona, we agreed that she would launch the lesson as I observed from within the group (that is, sitting among her kindergarteners, as in a coteaching situation, not removed from the group as is often the case in a formal evaluation or observation by a supervisor). This would allow Fiona to have experience implementing the curriculum with the opportunity for feedback after the lesson. She indicated that she was comfortable having me "jump in" if at any point I saw an important instructional move to be made that perhaps she was overlooking. Examples of coaching questions that can be used to define the focus and roles of coach and teacher are provided in the following box.

Defining Roles: Coach's Role and Teacher's Role

Below are questions that the coach may pose in a planning meeting to help define the roles that the coach and teacher will take on during the lesson.

- What is your professional learning focus for our coaching work together?
- What feedback or information from the lesson would be most useful in supporting your growth as a mathematics teacher?
- What will be my role during the lesson?
- What will be your role during the lesson?
- (If necessary) How would you like to introduce me to the students?
- (If necessary) Can I interject during the lesson?

Fiona's Case, Continued

THE LESSON

Sitting in a circle on the carpet, Fiona initiated the lesson with her group of 19 kindergarteners by holding up two trains, each made of eight snap cubes. One was a random arrangement of eight different colored snap cubes, while the other was arranged as an AB pattern using just red and white snap cubes. She asked the class to describe what they noticed about the two snap cube trains, specifically in terms of how they were the same and how they were different. She made a chart of "same" and "different" as students offered their observations and statements, such as "They both have eight cubes," "One has different colors but the other doesn't," and "They are straight."

Christina raised her hand, pointing to the train arranged as an AB pattern, and said confidently, "That one's a pattern!" Fiona recorded that observation on the chart paper and was ready to move on to others with their hands raised. From past experiences, I knew that this was an instance in which, as adults, we have a tendency to assume that the term *pattern* is being interpreted by a child in the same way as adults interpret it. We assume that they are paying attention to the important characteristics that make a pattern be a pattern, but in fact, we often realize that children have narrowly defined *pattern* for themselves or have not realized the defining characteristic of a pattern.

I wondered if Fiona would probe further here with questions to uncover Christina's understanding of the term *pattern*. But Fiona was focused on working through the same-different chart with the group; this is not uncommon for new teachers as they work hard to implement lessons for the first time. However, as a coach, I didn't want to lose the opportunity for Fiona to see the moments when a teacher needs to probe a child's thinking further to truly grasp a sense of the child's level of understanding. So I decided that this was a valuable moment to interject as a coach to model the probing questions that a teacher might put forth in response to Christina's statement:

KRW (to Christina, but aloud for the group and Fiona to hear):	What makes that train be a pattern?
Christina:	Because it has two colors and patterns always have two colors.

I could have probed further, but I didn't want to derail the lesson and I felt this modeled sufficiently for Fiona the type of probing that might follow a child's statement to gain some further insight into their thinking. I noted to myself that this would be something to come back to at the post-lesson conference. I let Fiona continue with the lesson launch and she then sent the students to work making other eight-cube trains at tables in the classroom with buckets of assorted colored snap cubes.

Fiona and I circulated as the children constructed their eight-cube trains. Most made trains of random arrangements initially. As the activity session went on, however, more and more began to construct some trains in patterned arrangements. The most common were AB pattern trains, but I also noticed Claire who had made a pattern in an ABC arrangement and Thomas and Sam who both had AAB patterns. Jonah used the trains of peers to build random arrangements, but he did work intently to make them all eight cubes long.

CHECKING IN

After 15 minutes of constructing eight-cube trains, I came up alongside Fiona. I wanted to check in with her before we gathered the group for the sorting of their trains. What had she noticed in her observations? While I had been observing the students myself, I was doing so with an eye toward coaching Fiona in her next steps.

Fiona had noticed the range of trains that the children had at their tables but she seemed very nervous and unsure how to orchestrate the whole-group sorting component of the session. I decided to offer to sit alongside her to cofacilitate the sorting discussion with her. She was still so new to the curriculum and this work with kindergarteners that I wanted to take this opportunity to guide her through the session in a manner that provided her with a model that the two of us could reference in future sessions. My offer seemed to put Fiona a bit more at ease. As she called the group to the rug, she asked each child to select one eight-cube train to bring to the discussion and she brought to the meeting an ABC pattern train she had constructed.

To begin the sorting discussion, Fiona placed the original random eight-cube arrangement on the rug to mark one pile and the original AB pattern train to mark another pile. Each child placed an eight-cube train in one of the two piles. Most placed their trains in the correct pile but two trains were placed in the pattern pile with errors in the patterns. After the last child placed her train in a pile, Fiona pulled her own ABC pattern train from behind her and showed it to the group. She asked the group to indicate which pile they thought she should put her train in. Some indicated the pattern pile while others indicated the random arrangement pile; some seemed unsure and hesitant to commit to one pile or the other.

MAKING THE MOVE

I could sense that Fiona was uncomfortable with the uncertainty from the children with regard to her ABC train. I decided that it would be appropriate for me to steer the discussion a bit at this point. I wanted to avoid pushing for a quick decision about the placement of Fiona's train; the children needed more time to examine the trains in the piles to be able to have a clear sense of the defining characteristics of each of the piles. I suggested to the group that we put Fiona's train in the middle of the two piles "just for now" so we could study the other piles first. That, I said, might give us new ideas that would help us put Fiona's train where it goes. The children were agreeable to this and seemed genuinely interested now in figuring out the placement of Fiona's train. As I looked over at Fiona, her intent and body language as I made this move conveyed a sense of engagement and interest in how I was facilitating the situation as well. I decided to continue as a model for her since I was not sure she had a sense of how to address this third pile that I had made.

I asked the group to first study the pattern pile:

KRW: Are there any trains in this pile that you are not sure about?

George pointed to Max's train.

A   B   C   A   B   A   B   C

I held the train up for the group to see and I asked for their thoughts; the responses were mixed. Most children were relying on the overall visual appearance of the train; it seemed to approximate the others in the "pattern" pile with its AB segments. I then asked the group to "read" several of the trains in the AB pattern pile. As I pointed to each cube in a train, the children said the color orally; they noticed that in these trains, their mouths seemed to "know" what should come next. I reminded them that Christina had used the math word *pattern* earlier in the math class and that a pattern lets us know what is coming next.

Now we returned to Max's train. As the children orally "read" the color of each cube in the train, several began to fill in the missing piece of the ABC pattern midway through the train. They realized that what sounded right was not what they saw in the train. Max stood up after we "read" the train twice and insisted that he knew what needed to be changed.

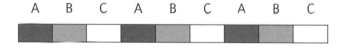

A   B   C   A   B   C   A   B   C

His train was now nine cubes long but that didn't seem to bother the others; instead, there was greater agreement that Max's train now did belong in the pile of trains that had an AB pattern because "your mouth knows what's coming next."

Haley turned then to Fiona's ABC train that was still in its own pile in the middle of the rug. "So that goes with these!" she said, pointing to the pile of pattern trains that we had just examined closely. Others in the group agreed, noting that it was the same as Max's but with different colors. It is interesting that there were two other ABC patterns in the pile already but it was not until we orally compared the trains that the group as a whole was convinced. I closed this sorting time with a question for the group to think about for the next day:

KRW: I notice that some of these trains we are calling patterns have more than two colors. Christina had said before that she thought patterns always have two colors. So what do you think about this now? Can a pattern have three colors? Think about that, and we'll save these trains for tomorrow.

Fiona brought the session to a close with directions to store the sorted piles and the other trains that students had made but left on their tables. These would all be available to continue the pattern discussion and experience the next day.

THE DEBRIEF MEETING

I was fortunate to be able to meet with Fiona immediately following the class lesson; she brought her students to their art class and then returned to the classroom for our conversation. The proximity of this meeting to the lesson was valuable in that the students' thinking and teacher's moves were fresh in our minds still. However, there is also value in waiting until the end of the day or even the next day to have a postlesson discussion or debrief meeting. The interval of time allows both the coach and teacher to reflect independently on the lesson. As a coach, I find that I am then able to craft and prepare probing questions for the meeting in a more strategic way. Both circumstances can be effective; what is critical is that the debrief meeting *does* occur at some point. Observation or demonstration alone is not enough in coaching.

As Fiona sat down next to me, I paused to let her gather her thoughts. Before I could begin, she jumped in:

Fiona: So what did you think?

It was tempting to begin sharing my thoughts and perspectives on the lesson, but I knew that as a coach my role was to first push Fiona to reflect on the lesson.

KRW: Well, that is what I want to ask you. What did *you* think?

Fiona's response was quick, too quick really.

Fiona: I think it went well. I think it was good.

I waited. "Uh-huh," I replied. Then I paused again as I looked at Fiona. I reminded myself: wait time, eye contact. I waited some more. Then I said, "Tell me more." Fiona realized that I was waiting for her to be more specific in her reflection and response.

Fiona: It was really helpful to hear how you asked questions. I guess I probably need to ask more questions.

This seemed like a nice entry into some of the key moments in the lesson that were ripe for our coaching conversation. I wanted to continue this thread but push Fiona to be more explicit.

KRW: Can you give an example of what you mean? What were those questions?

Fiona: Like when Christina said the train was a pattern, I was just thinking that was it. That she knew what a pattern is. But then you asked her to explain it more, and I realized that maybe she didn't understand it as well as I thought.

KRW: And when we asked some more questions, we found out that she had an interesting perception of pattern. She thought of patterns as two colors.

Fiona: I have a couple of kids like that who can speak really well, and they seem like they are really with it. But now I am wondering if maybe sometimes I need to push them to explain it a little more.

I was pleased with what she was noting and confirmed this for her.

KRW: It was important for us to hear Christina and know how she was thinking, and most likely others were thinking that way. By knowing that, we could have them bump up against that idea in the meeting at the end of the lesson.

EXPANDING THE DISCUSSION

Fiona next shifted her reflections to Max.

Fiona: I was watching Max closely when you were holding up his train and asking others to think about it. He's kind of sensitive, but he seemed OK in the end with it. I wasn't really sure how that would work to have kids agree or disagree.

It was interesting that the conversation was now moving to issues that are relevant to the overall classroom culture and environment. This reminded me that Fiona is a first-year teacher still establishing her vision of the classroom climate. I found myself drawing here not on any knowledge base specific to mathematics but rather on my own years and experiences as a classroom teacher.

KRW: Part of this is setting the climate in the classroom and, from the beginning, letting children know that you expect them to listen to each other. It's about letting them know that in math class it's OK to disagree but there are appropriate and respectful ways to disagree. And that you can make revisions to your work. That was more of what we were doing than saying Max was wrong; it was about using his work as a chance for all of us to think together.

I made a note to myself that this was an important dimension of the effective mathematics classroom for us to continue to examine and develop together over the course of the year. It is not specific to this lesson alone or even this unit but rather would be valuable to discuss at any coaching meeting in terms of establishing the shared understanding in the classroom of what mathematicians do and how they discuss and develop ideas with one another respectfully.

PUSHING THE DISCUSSION FURTHER

Now I wanted to pose some questions to continue to probe and push reflection for Fiona.

KRW: At what point in the lesson do you think children were learning the most?

Fiona: I don't think the beginning really made much sense to them. But I think what made it click was classifying the trains at the end into the two piles. That was really good.

KRW: And that is where it was helpful that we had heard what some of the students like Christina had said. We could choose trains at the rug that would lend themselves to uncovering the idea of pattern carefully. That is why, when you put out your ABC train, I diverted the conversation a bit to put it in the middle. Did you notice the split in the class's thinking about that one?

Fiona: Yep, I guess I wasn't expecting that. Or at least, I hadn't thought about what I would do when they actually didn't all agree!

KRW: What I was worried about was that if we just moved right to agreeing with those who said it was a pattern they would not have really ever established how to distinguish a pattern from another arrangement. Even though Claire's train and Max's revised train were both ABC patterns, they weren't making the connection.

Fiona: Right. I could see that hearing it for some really made it work. Like I could see Max when you read his, he realized that it was easy to make his be a pattern. He couldn't see it at first with the cubes, but he could when he heard you read it aloud.

With this exchange, I had shifted my role in the conversation from one of listening and prompting Fiona for self-reflection to one of more actively steering the conversation and offering my own observations and perspectives. I also wanted to be explicit with Fiona about my own thinking and purposeful decisions made during the group sorting of the trains. Being explicit about these decisions would model for her the type of thinking that a teacher undertakes when facilitating a classroom discussion and would also model for her that this was not simply a matter of instinct but rather grounded in the goal of the lesson and the student thinking that had been made evident in the classroom.

For a moment, I worried that I was talking too much. It is all too easy to fall into the trap of talking too much in these postlesson conversations—especially when there are so many observations that I am excited to share with a teacher—but here a nice balance seemed to be struck. The responses from Fiona indicated that she was not merely listening passively as I spoke. Rather, she was actively making connections to her own observations and there was a shared ownership of puzzling over and making sense of the children's thinking in the lesson.

I wanted to hear her thoughts about next steps, but our meeting time was over. I left her with a few thoughts as to how to open tomorrow's class with that question regarding three-color patterns. Our meeting time came to a close.

TAKING A CLOSER LOOK

What made this debrief meeting so satisfying as a coach? It was the balance that seemed to be maintained in the coaching interactions. The conversation flowed from general reflections to a focus on student work and thinking to discussion of specific moments in the lesson. Figure 3.2 outlines this flow of a debrief meeting.

There was also a balance of prompts for teacher self-reflection and more explicit coaching observations and suggestions about the teaching and learning in the classroom. There were moments in the meeting that pushed Fiona to reflect on the lesson for herself. As tempting as it was to

Figure 3.2 A Debrief Meeting Flowchart

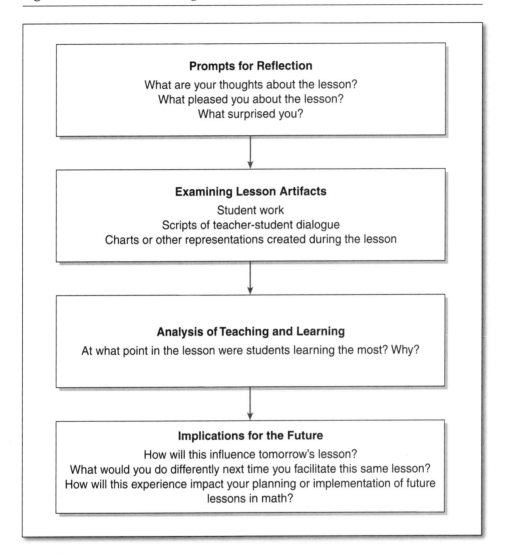

jump right in with my perspectives when she sat down at the table and asked for my thoughts on the lesson, I knew that a critical role of the coach is to serve as a mediator between the teacher and her reflections on a lesson. It was important to push Fiona to first reflect for herself on the lesson, to give the wait time that implies an expectation of deep reflection on the part of the teacher and to push further still for more specificity in the reflection with such probes as, "Can you give an example of . . . ?"

There were moments of coaching questions that continued to facilitate the reflection but in a more focused manner. These are questions not necessarily specific to Fiona's case; these are questions that transcend coaching meetings in that they move the reflection and conversation to new levels. Questions such as "At what point in the lesson do you think students were learning the most?" push reflection in a way that teachers have not often considered before, while questions such as "Where will you go next with this?" prompt a teacher to synthesize and apply the observations and reflection from a lesson to inform the instruction and plan for the next day in a facilitated environment with a coach.

There are still other debriefing questions that a coach may use that can prompt a teacher to reflect on practice more broadly. For instance, a coach may conclude a coaching session by posing the question, "How will your learning from this lesson impact the way you are thinking about other math lessons you teach?" This question is intended to prompt a teacher to generalize learning beyond one coaching experience and apply the implications to future instructional planning and practice. Such questions also imply the expectation that the coaching experience has a sustained, long-term impact.

There were also moments of more explicit steering evident in the debrief meeting with Fiona. This came in the form of paraphrasing and elaborating on the points Fiona raised or questions she posed. It also came in the form of sharing some of my own observations from the lesson and in offering some direct suggestions or recommendations for Fiona. These coach observations, suggestions, and recommendations are much more explicit and direct than the prompts for teacher reflection heard early in the debrief meeting with Fiona, but they are often the catalysts for teacher growth and next steps in terms of creating a shared focus and agenda for the coaching work.

THE NEED FOR VARIATIONS IN THE COACHING CYCLE

This coaching cycle with Fiona was an established weekly sequence with her willingness—encouraged through her building principal—to set aside prep time for our planning session and debrief meeting. In some cases, districts or building administrators who are committed to supporting the coaching work being undertaken in their schools may provide coverage or release time for teachers to meet with the coach to ensure that the integrity of the coaching cycle is maintained. Other teachers who have sought out the support and collaboration of a coach may offer their time before or after school or during lunch periods to meet with the coach for these conversations.

But the reality that surfaces in other buildings or coaching situations is that time is a scarce commodity in schools and even very willing or committed teachers may find it difficult to give time on a regular basis for both a prelesson and postlesson meeting with the coach. The coach then must determine variations of the coaching cycle that can ensure productive coaching opportunities but within the parameters of time constraints. During my years as a coach, I have encountered different time constraints and have had to undertake my own sort of action research in terms of variations of the coaching cycle that can be valuable and satisfying not only for the teacher but for the coach as well.

Some teachers are willing to commit their time to the intensity of coaching sessions when the duration of the work is defined. For instance, rather than asking one teacher to work with me in a coaching partnership for the entire school year, I may suggest that a teacher commit to a weekly coaching cycle of planning, lesson, and postlesson dialogue for the length of one specific unit in the district mathematics curriculum. This has proven to be well received by elementary teachers who find the year-long commitment daunting in light of the other demands on their time. The defined duration of a unit allows them to recognize that their commitment is finite, so they are more willing to protect our time together during that unit. There is an intensity to the coaching cycle then; rather than biweekly or monthly meetings, the coaching for the unit is weekly or even several consecutive days each week to support the development of mathematical concepts and ideas from one day to the next. This allows for continuity and focused work together, particularly in the case of teachers with whom I have already built trust and rapport through past years' work or team meetings at the building. Although the commitment is made for a selected unit only, I often find that teachers will ask to continue to work together in future units as well; they have experienced firsthand the impact of the coaching work and so return asking for more.

Technology offers another means to overcome time obstacles in the coaching cycle if both parties are comfortable with virtual dialogue. E-mail can be used to check in with a teacher regarding plans for an upcoming lesson if a full planning meeting cannot be held. Some teachers keep an electronic log or journal to capture their reflections on a lesson; some coaches do the same. Collaborative documents, such as Google Docs, and blogs are also ways for the coach and teacher to engage in shared dialogue online when time constraints are a factor.

If a debrief meeting cannot be scheduled for several days after a lesson, I find it important to send along a set of reflection questions immediately after the lesson. I ask the teacher to use those questions to guide his or her reflection on the lesson and to bring those thoughts to our postlesson discussion; this helps to ensure that the teacher's reflection occurs while the lesson is still fresh in his or her mind and these reflections, along with student work or other artifacts from the lesson, become a springboard for the debrief meeting when it is held. This is particularly helpful when schedules require that one meeting with a teacher serve as both the debrief discussion from the previous lesson and the planning meeting for the next lesson.

Other efficiencies of time may come in the form of discussing upcoming unit lessons with grade-level teams rather than with individual teachers. More and more, schools are establishing schedules that provide weekly common planning time for grade-level teams to plan collaboratively; a coach could attend and facilitate a team meeting to unpack the mathematics, student thinking and misconceptions, and implications for instruction. This would allow the planning meeting to occur as a collaborative experience with the team, followed by coach visits to several different classrooms during the lesson. The postlesson conversation could then occur individually with those teachers, or it could include individual e-mail reflections and a group debrief at another team meeting. This curtails some opportunities for the coach to address specific individual needs on the team, but it does promote the development of a community of learners on a grade-level team as they grow to examine practice and student thinking together and share perspectives with one another in this facilitated setting.

Finally, there may be instances in which a teacher will not or cannot commit to meeting outside of class time and no team meeting time is available as an option either. I have struggled with this as a coach. Do I still schedule in-class time with that teacher? Or do I refuse to work with a teacher who will not set aside time to meet? I have experienced situations of feeling very awkward because no meaningful dialogue happened before or after the lesson; the work felt very disjointed and wasteful from a time perspective. If I can at least stop in a teacher's room prior to the lesson to ask him or her to share with me what the lesson will address and what the teacher is focusing on in terms of his or her own growth, then I can focus my observation and notes in the classroom accordingly. I will not agree to coteach or model a lesson without a planning meeting together to ensure shared ownership of the lesson, but observing with a teacher-selected focus in a classroom can occur effectively with just a brief checking in. The debrief dialogue in some format, however, is critical—and so nonnegotiable in terms of time—from the perspective of coaching as a vehicle for teacher growth.

KEYS TO THE COACHING CYCLE

The coaching cycle is a powerful structure for coaches to employ with the teachers they work with. It is easy to be misled, however, to believe that it is the structure of the coaching cycle itself—the prelesson or planning meeting, the classroom lesson experience, and the postlesson or debrief meeting—that renders coaching work effective. It is not the structure itself that will yield results; planning meetings, lessons, and debrief meetings can occur over and over again with little impact if they are not approached purposefully by the coach. Closer analysis of each component of the coaching cycle, as we undertook in this chapter, reveals critical elements that render the coaching cycle effective:

- Unpacking the mathematics
- Identifying a shared focus
- Grounding discussions in student work and student thinking

- Questioning to prompt teacher reflection and analysis
- Steering the teacher toward new ideas or perspectives when appropriate

Keeping these points in mind allows a coach to harness the full potential not only of a formal coaching cycle but of any coaching moment with a teacher.

While a full coaching cycle may not always be possible for a coach, it is possible for a coach to develop deep understanding of what these core elements of coaching entail and to frame all coaching interactions and moments with teachers with these elements in mind. The list is not meant to be exhaustive. It is purposely limited in the number of elements put forth to provide focal points for the coach in designing coaching sessions. The chapters that follow will unpack several of these core elements still further.

Questions for Reflecting and Linking to Practice

1. Select or create a set of planning meeting questions to pose in a coaching session with a teacher. How can these questions be crafted to provide a guiding frame for your coaching meeting and yet be open-ended enough to adjust based on the teacher's responses?

2. Brainstorm the range of roles that might be taken on by a coach during the classroom lesson component of the coaching cycle. Note explicitly how each of these roles can be harnessed, directly or indirectly, to support the development and professional growth of the teacher. What are some of the pitfalls to avoid in these roles?

3. Consider how the coaching cycle is or might be carried out in your district and the challenges that may emerge. What elements of the coaching cycle are nonnegotiable as you coach teachers?

PART II

Tools for Coaching

4

Using Curriculum

I remember spending hours every night as a first-year mathematics coach pouring over the teacher unit guides at each grade level. My classroom experience had been primarily in the lower elementary grades, so I focused on learning about the curriculum and development of mathematical ideas in the upper elementary grades. I needed to feel comfortable not only with a given lesson that a teacher might be implementing in a classroom but also on the overall development of mathematical ideas over time, from one session to the next across a unit, to truly be able to support the teacher in navigating a unit and making instructional decisions in the classroom.

The teacher unit guides were a professional development resource for me as a coach and I quickly realized that they also could be a powerful tool for supporting teacher learning in coaching sessions. The guides are resources that teachers turn to every day, and they provide a common ground for discussion of mathematical ideas. The work of the coach is to support the teacher in viewing these teacher guides not as a collection of classroom activities but as a tool for navigating the curriculum of mathematical ideas that students are to develop over time. But how does a coach guide a teacher to view curriculum through this lens? How can a coach use the curriculum, and student interactions with the curriculum, as a tool for improving teaching and learning in the classroom?

DEFINING THE MEANING OF CURRICULUM

It is important to note here that curriculum can be defined in many ways. Curriculum can be the written curriculum that articulates what students will know, understand, and be able to do at the end of a unit of study or at the end of a grade. Most often, a core delivery system—a purchased program of resources, learning experiences, or a textbook—supports the implementation of the written curriculum in the classroom. More and more, curriculum developers recognize that curriculum resources and teacher guides can be designed not only to serve as instructional materials for students but also as professional learning tools for teachers. Some curriculum resources now include professional notes about mathematics content, about research related to how children learn mathematics, or about pedagogy. These materials are clearly intended by the curriculum developers to be used by teachers as professional development tools, and a mathematics coach can facilitate text-based discussions and dialogue with a teacher using these resources.

While the written curriculum may be the intended curriculum, there is also the case of the enacted curriculum. This is the curriculum that actually plays out in the classroom. It is the sequence and pacing of concepts and skills that are addressed in the classroom and the resources and tools actually used in the classroom. I would extend this further to argue that it is also the dynamic shaping of curriculum that occurs as both teacher and students interact with the content of curriculum in its implementation.

As I write about curriculum in this chapter, I take the perspective that as a coach all dimensions of curriculum need to be considered as possible leverage points. Unpacking the written curriculum provides opportunities for discussions about the mathematical ideas being taught. Artifacts of the enacted curriculum, such as teachers' charts as they launch a lesson, lists of student conjectures emerging from an activity, or scripts of student dialogue, can also be used to ground discussions about pedagogy and student learning in math class. This chapter examines instances in which the coach harnesses curriculum materials—and the student artifacts that result from the implementation of curriculum in the classroom—as a vehicle for dialogue between the teacher and coach, with the professional growth of the teacher as the aim.

Case: Talking About Curriculum ∞ Sue, Grade 2

In this case, I needed to respond to a teacher's request for resources to supplement the district's Grade 2 geometry curriculum. As I reflected on ways to respond, I realized that the underlying issue to address was the teacher's understanding of the big ideas of mathematics and how children develop these ideas. My meeting with this teacher demonstrated how powerful vertical conversations about the mathematics in the grades before and after can be in coaching.

SETTING THE STAGE

I felt extremely uneasy as I sat with a pile of mathematics resources beside me. I was planning for my meeting with Sue, a veteran second-grade teacher in the district and team leader at her school. I flipped through the pages of several resources, glancing at the geometry activities that were described. Last week, Sue came to me requesting that we look at resources to supplement the geometry unit of the Grade 2 curriculum; she felt the new curriculum units implemented three years ago were not substantial enough for students. We scheduled a meeting for the next morning to tackle this work.

But as I sat planning, I felt concerned that the meeting would be spent selecting geometry activities with little thought as to how the activities would support the development of geometric ideas over time. I feared the activities would be chosen for "activity's sake" alone. How would that support Sue in thinking deeply about the mathematics and development of children's geometric ideas?

With that fear in mind, I put aside the additional resource books and turned to my copy of the Grade 2 core geometry unit of the district curriculum. Though I was familiar with the unit and had read its components previously, I read through the front material that outlined the mathematical ideas of the unit again. I reread several of the session overviews and supporting materials. I became more and more convinced that my feelings of uneasiness were for good reason. In fact, I felt convinced that the unit itself was a rich unit that addressed not only the properties of shapes but also the decomposing and recomposing of space. It considered the different attributes of a shape that could be measured (height, area, etc.). It presented important connections between number and geometry in its building of rectangular arrays, and it set a foundation for the fraction work that children would continue in the years ahead.

Why was it that this unit seemed so rich to me yet not to other Grade 2 teachers such as Sue? It seemed to me that this pointed to the need for these teachers to develop a deeper understanding of the mathematics in the unit itself and in the experiences they were implementing from the unit in the classroom. If they looked closely at the mathematics emphases in each session and focused their questions in the classroom with an eye on the mathematics embedded in the lesson, the unit could be incredibly rich.

Perhaps I was also able to see the richness of the unit because I was familiar with the geometry units at the other grade levels. I could readily see the connections between the second-grade unit, what came before in the first-grade geometry unit, and what was ahead for children in the third-grade mathematics curriculum and beyond. It seemed to me that Sue and her teammates needed to gain a sense of the larger context in which the Grade 2 geometry work occurred.

So by the end of the evening, my plan for the meeting had changed completely. I no longer planned to spend the next morning flipping through resource guides with Sue to select a packet of new geometry activities. I wanted to support Sue in developing a lens through which she could recognize for herself the rich mathematics of the Grade 2 work.

MAKING THE MOVE

I arrived carrying the pile of resource books that had remained all but untouched during my planning the night before. Why did I bring these if I did not think they were the most meaningful direction for us to follow in terms of developing a mathematical lens? I carried them with me because, as I sat down with Sue, I wanted her to know that I had heard her request the week before about wanting to look at other available resources. She was excited to see the books, and it seemed to set a comfortable tone for our meeting as she began flipping through the pages of one.

Then I began the meeting by saying that I had gathered these resources for us to use if necessary but that, before we began to look for additional activities to include in the unit, I wondered if perhaps we should first "take stock." By this, I meant that I wondered if we should first identify the big ideas of geometry that are already addressed in the current district unit and what we saw as the big ideas of geometry that we wanted second graders to have experience with. I used that very language: "I wonder if . . . ." I also mentioned that before we poured over the additional resources for more activities I thought it might be helpful to look through the geometry units at the first- and third-grade levels to make certain that we were not simply duplicating experiences that children would be having in those grades. I had brought copies of those with me as well.

I held my breath as I awaited Sue's response. I hoped she would trust me in following this direction. I hoped that in undertaking this work she would come to recognize for herself the richness of the district geometry unit for Grade 2. She could then arrive at a decision for herself as to whether or not additional activities were needed at this time for the unit. She agreed that stepping back for a moment to look at the mathematics of the unit seemed to make sense.

LOOK WHO'S TALKING

In the time that we had together to talk, we were only able to talk about a very small part of the unit. Sue immediately began talking about the lesson that she had just undertaken that week with her students, the "sorting cards" work. She talked extensively and openly about how this was the third year she had used the program and about how much better she felt at being able to facilitate the discussions in her classroom as children sorted a set of cards that pictures a variety of geometric figures. She talked about how much more her students took from the experience this year as compared to years past. She attributed this to being more familiar herself with the lesson, the manner in which children may think about the shapes, and what questions to ask to further the conversation or challenge students' thinking. She also made reference to research I had presented to her team at a recent grade-level meeting regarding children's development of geometric thinking. She talked about how this had informed her questioning and her ability to make sense of student responses.

It was interesting how little talking I had to do at this point; now that Sue had the opportunity to reflect on her students' learning and their experiences with the curriculum, she had much to say. Sue said, "I didn't realize how many ideas about shapes my students could talk about from the sorting cards until this year. You almost have to know how to read between the lines in the teacher's guide. . . . It's like it's all there but you just need to find it. I didn't see it all at first, but after using it in my classroom for three years, I am finding more and more in it." For Sue, the experience of using the curriculum for the past three years and now having a coach to prompt her reflection and discussion of the work in the classroom was a significant piece of professional development.

Sue began then to ask questions about the two-dimensional geometry experiences in the third-grade curriculum. She was particularly interested in hearing about the manner in which the area model of fractions introduced in second grade is carried forward and built upon in third grade. It seemed to put her at ease in the sense that she was able to set more appropriate expectations for her students in this work knowing that they would be building on their experiences the following year. Previously, she had felt the fraction work was not pushing them far enough and fast enough; now she could see the importance of setting this solid foundation for the work in later years. It was as if her second-grade work now had a context rather than existing in isolation.

Our meeting time came to a close much too soon. We had only begun to touch on the mathematics of the unit. As we left, Sue indicated that she felt it was important for all of the second-grade teachers to meet together to discuss the unit in order to fully uncover the mathematics that is embedded in each session. I left the meeting feeling extremely satisfied. The work had been Sue's. I had put forth questions and comments to scaffold our work and turn it in a direction that was much different than what Sue had originally requested, but it was a direction that allowed Sue to realize for herself the richness of the unit. This led her to have ownership of the work and ownership of the learning.

TAKING A CLOSER LOOK

The meeting with Sue turned from a focus on a collection of activities to a study of the mathematical ideas that students were developing in geometry. This required intentional steering on my part as the coach. To steer the conversation in this new direction, I used the language "I wonder if . . ." as noted earlier. This language was intentional; I wanted to convey the message that this was about us exploring mathematical ideas together. It seemed to allow Sue to suspend her desire to look at other resources for the moment.

What brought Sue to uncover the mathematics was her reflection on the work of her students in the classroom as they interacted with the curriculum experiences. She recognized that as she listened to student thinking and provided them opportunities to discuss their ideas, she was becoming more aware of the power of the learning experiences and the geometric ideas that they brought out for students. This speaks not only to the importance of a rich curriculum that provides such opportunities for students to communicate their mathematical ideas but also to the importance of developing the ear of the teacher for student thinking. In this case, the coach simply listened and let Sue reflect on her new insights for herself; in other cases, a coach may need to use more probing questions or more direct articulation of the mathematical ideas embedded in the unit.

Finally, the links to the first- and third-grade geometry units allowed Sue to place her teaching as a piece of ongoing development of ideas for her students. Often, curriculum sessions for teachers—particularly when adopting or implementing a new curriculum unit—bring together teachers at a grade level to examine the mathematics of that grade specifically. Teachers remain focused on their own grade level, and often in the first year or two of implementation, this is a necessary focus for teachers. But attention then needs to be given to the vertical articulation of curriculum across the grades; children experience curriculum as a K–12 experience. Unfortunately, teachers rarely have the opportunity to consider the curriculum in this way. Opportunities to examine how mathematical ideas build from one year to the next can deepen teachers' understanding of how their own grade-level work fits into the broader development of a child's mathematics learning.

USING THE CURRICULUM AS A COACHING TOOL

This use of curriculum as a tool for coaching teachers can be done in a variety of ways. The teacher guides themselves are tools for the coach in these conversations, as was the case in my meeting with Sue in this chapter. But other tools that emerge indirectly from the curriculum can also be used both with individual teachers and with teams of teachers. Several are discussed below.

Classroom Scripts

Scripting is often associated with supervision and evaluation practices; administrators conducting teacher observations will often script the class lesson and then include this script as part of the evaluation report. In my work as a coach, I have found scripting to be a very powerful tool for recording the student thinking and dialogue that occurs in the classroom. After scripting a segment of a class session on a notepad while in the classroom, I will often type the script and share it with the teacher as an artifact of the classroom lesson. Because the scripts focus on what children are doing and saying in the classroom, I have found that teachers often appreciate them. Such classroom discussion often occurs so quickly in the moment that it is hard for a teacher to recreate it later in his or her own mind exactly for reflection. Teachers appreciate having powerful classroom learning moments captured on paper for them to look back on and recall the thinking contributed by specific students. Just as Sue described what she could reconstruct of her students' thinking related to the sorting cards discussion during the meeting, classroom scripts allow teacher and coach together to examine and reflect on the student thinking from a lesson.

As I share the script with a teacher during a coaching meeting, the script provides a springboard into conversation about the mathematics learning that is evident in the script. What is it that students understand about the topic under discussion? What is the evidence of that understanding? What seems confusing to these students? What are they grappling with in their conversations or work? A script may also be used to capture the work that students share during a classroom discussion so it serves as a set of work samples to discuss. Figure 4.1 is one example of a script of student addition strategies that I recorded during a second-grade discussion time; it provided the entry point for my conversation with the teacher about the range of strategies his students used, the number sense that each demonstrated, and the next steps for students in their development of computational fluency.

It may seem odd to include this discussion of classroom scripts in a chapter devoted to curriculum, but from the perspective of coaching, classroom scripts represent the intersection of curriculum and students, and from the perspective of curriculum, classroom scripts can capture the interaction of students with curriculum. Scripts bring together curriculum and students in a manner that allows learning to be examined with the teacher and discussed in terms of implications for instruction. These

Figure 4.1   Sample Script of Student Strategies From a Second-Grade Classroom

There are 31 cars and 14 buses in the school parking lot.
How many cars and buses are there in all?

*As Bob's second graders shared their strategies for solving this story problem,
I recorded the work they showed and the explanation they gave to the group.*

Charles

$$31 \quad + \quad 14$$
$$40 + 5 = 45$$

"I put the 3 tens and the 1 ten to make 40, and I took the 1 leftover from the 3 tens and the 4 leftover from the 14 and got 5. Then I plussed 40 and 5 to make 45."

Melissa

$$31 \quad + \quad 14$$
$$30 + 1 + 10 + 4 = 45$$

"I knew 30 + 10 is 40, and 1 + 4 is 5, so it's 45."

Katrina

$$31 + 14 = 45$$

"I did 31 and then I counted 14 more on my fingers."

Jackie

$$31 \quad + \quad 14$$
$$4 \quad 5 = 45$$

"I broke down the 10's, then the 1's."

Susannah

$$31 + 14 = 45$$

"I know that 30 + 14 = 44, and +1 more is 45."

David

$$31 \quad + \quad 14$$
$$34 \quad + \quad 11$$

"I took the 30 from 31 and the 4 from 14 to make 34. Then I did 30 and 10 to make 40 and 4 and 1 for 5."

scripts serve as a neutral ground for discussing the implementation of curriculum because they focus on student learning, the shared goal of teacher and coach. Samples of student work from a lesson or assessment can be used in a similar manner, and many protocols have been developed to structure such a use of classroom learning artifacts in an objective manner. The Web site www.lasw.org/protocols.html is one resource for coaches looking for protocols when using student work with teachers.

Doing the Math

At the elementary level, it is often assumed that the mathematics content is familiar to a teacher. But for most teachers, their experiences in mathematics were those that they experienced in elementary school themselves, often with a focus on arithmetic and rote computational procedures. Many teachers know *how* to do the mathematics but this is much different than understanding the discipline of mathematics or the manner in which mathematical ideas build over time and connect. What's more, many elementary mathematics programs embed activities involving manipulatives and games as core instructional experiences for students; these are powerful experiences for students but can be diminished to activity-for-activity's sake if teachers are not clear on the mathematical focus and intent of the experience.

All of this speaks to the power of teachers doing the mathematics that is embedded in the curriculum they are teaching. In some instances, teachers might undertake a piece of mathematics related to the curriculum but at an adult level. This provides them the opportunity to unpack the big ideas of mathematics for themselves and to engage in the work of being a learner in a manner that parallels how we hope students engage in the mathematics in the classroom.

In other instances, teachers might do the actual activity described in a teacher manual and reflect on the mathematics of the activity, asking the question, "What's the math?" The discussion can lead to an analysis of the mathematical ideas embedded in the activity and teachers can then consider how to pose questions to bring that mathematics forward during the class session for students. As teachers do the mathematics of a unit for themselves, they uncover the importance or complexity of the ideas students are developing. They gain insights into the misconceptions or pitfalls that they may encounter from students in the classroom and can plan proactively to develop questions that will bring these forward for discussion.

Doing the math can be undertaken by a coach and teacher one-on-one at a coaching meeting as they examine curriculum together, or it may occur in group meetings of teachers facilitated by a coach. What is critical is that a teacher considers not merely what students will "do" in the classroom as part of a curricular experience, but also what mathematics the experience is intended to bring forth for students to examine and learn. Selecting pivotal or keystone lessons in a curriculum unit—lessons that capture a critical moment in the development of a mathematical idea in a given unit of study—as the focus of study for a coaching meeting or a meeting with a group of teachers is one way for coaches to leverage the curriculum materials in this manner.

Agendas for Learning

Perhaps the most common instance in which a coach may use curriculum resources as a professional development tool with teachers is that of unit overviews or curriculum support during the implementation of new curriculum or a new program. Some strict models may not consider this coaching given that it occurs in a group setting and often plays out in a manner that is more in the realm of curriculum training. But the reality of many coaching positions is that a district expects a coach to take on this curriculum responsibility with teams of teachers as well and so it can be useful to consider how to best leverage the opportunities. Indeed, meeting with a team of teachers for these curriculum conversations can be a less threatening way for teachers to begin to work with a coach, gain a sense of the expertise the coach brings to the work, and form a trusting relationship with the coach. Often, following group curriculum meetings, teachers will be more open to a coach coming into their classrooms or working with the coach individually. In this way, these meetings can be efficient, effective entry points into one-on-one coaching work.

Critical to the success of these group or team curriculum meetings with teachers is the structure of these meetings to ensure that teams are examining curriculum with a focus on the mathematics and student development of mathematical ideas, not merely on the activities of the unit. Using an agenda for learning can frame the meeting to ensure this focus. A sample agenda for one curriculum unit overview for a Grade 1 team is presented in Figure 4.2. It indicates that the discussion will build from the mathematics to the evidence of student learning and then to the learning experiences that support this learning; this is in contrast to turning page by page through a unit to examine the activities (which is how I used to present unit overviews to teachers). Although this sample agenda is from a meeting that focused on one unit overview, a similar agenda format can be used for vertical alignment meetings designed to illuminate cross-grade connections across a strand of mathematics for a group of teachers as well.

The agenda is as much for the benefit of the teachers as it is for the coach; it keeps everyone aware of the purposeful manner in which they are deconstructing the unit or curriculum strand. The goal is that teachers will themselves internalize this approach to curriculum and ask themselves a similar set of questions each time they are implementing a unit or even a class session. In this way, the agenda is a coaching tool intended to support the growth of the teacher.

KEYS TO COACHING WITH CURRICULUM

As math coaches shape teachers' understanding of curriculum, they strive to develop a lens that views curriculum as a landscape of mathematical understandings, concepts, and skills—not as a collection of activities

Figure 4.2   Agenda for Grade 1 Mathematics Unit Overview Meeting

Date: December 10	Time: 12:50–1:50 PM	Location: Donna's room	
	Facilitator: Kris	Timekeeper: Ellen	Minutes: Joanne

Outcome	Process	Prework	Time
What do we want children to understand, know, and be able to do (with respect to data analysis)?	**Jigsaw:** • About the Math, pp. 10–13 (4 sections) • Classroom Routines, p. 16 (and Implementation Guide)	Read **Unit 4, Mathematics in the Unit,** pp. 10–13, and Classroom Routines, p. 16 (and Implementation Guide)	25 minutes
How will we know what children have learned?	**Benchmark/ assessment overview** **Text talk:** Unit benchmarks, p. 15 **Pair and share:** Walk through teacher notes, including assessment pages and student work sample pages, p. 121		15 minutes
What experiences will support children in this learning?	**Post-it tag unit learning experiences** • Session overview chart • Quick surveys (see attached notes) • Number string equations, pp. 55, 93 • Coins, in Classroom Routines, encourage coin sorting in Inv. 1 • Exemplars		20 minutes

(Fosnot, Dolk, & Cameron, 2001). It becomes important then for a coach to use the curriculum itself and the artifacts of student learning from their interaction with the curriculum as a tool for deepening teacher understanding and practice. Rather than bringing more and more resources to a teacher, a coach must first step back and harness the curriculum that the teacher works with every day, whether in the form of teacher unit guides or district curriculum documents. This is not to say that a coach may never share new resources for a teacher to consider implementing with students, but there must be caution not to simply present to a teacher a buffet of activities that lack coherence or purpose in terms of deepening understandings. This use of curriculum by the coach can ensure that the curriculum is not merely a vehicle for student learning but for teacher learning as well.

Some texts or programs used as the delivery system for curriculum in a district may not offer many obvious professional development tools. Similarly, some district curricula may provide a list of narrowly defined skills to be taught but provide little emphasis on the development of mathematical thinking, reasoning, problem solving, or communication. In these instances, the coach must find ways to deepen the mathematical conversations with a teacher by steering those conversations toward the concepts that underlie what may otherwise be presented as a rote, procedural skill or algorithm; the mathematical content knowledge of the coach is critical in this regard. Also, the coach must look for opportunities in the classroom to make children's mathematical ideas visible, perhaps by posing high-level questions to students in the classroom either to the whole group or to pairs or individuals within earshot of the teacher. Though these questions may not be written in the teacher unit guide or textbook, they serve to make student thinking public and ensure that there is student thinking for the teacher and coach to talk about at a coaching meeting.

Curriculum as a Coaching Tool

Strategies for using curriculum as a coaching tool include the following:

- Study existing curriculum materials collaboratively at coaching meetings with a **focus on the mathematics** intended for student learning
- Examine **cross-grade connections** and **vertical alignment** of curriculum in coaching discussions
- Use **scripts** to examine the interaction of students with curriculum
- Engage teachers in **doing the mathematics** for themselves
- Use **agendas for learning** that focus team meetings on the mathematics and development of mathematical ideas within a unit or across a strand

Questions for Reflecting and Linking to Practice

1. What new insights does this chapter provide with regard to how you might use your district curriculum or artifacts from the classroom in future coaching work?

2. Consider the script presented in Figure 4.1. How might you use this script with a teacher in a coaching meeting to steer the conversation toward mathematics of the second-grade curriculum and next steps for student learning?

3. As noted in this chapter, some districts may have a curriculum that has not been clearly articulated or lacks balance between conceptual and procedural knowledge for students. If that is the case, how might you find artifacts that illustrate students' mathematical thinking to use as springboards for curriculum conversations in coaching sessions with teachers?

5

The Role of Questioning

The role of questioning in teaching is evident. Thoughtful, purposeful questions from a teacher can prompt children to clarify, explain, extend, and reflect upon their thinking. This questioning also provides teachers with a window into a child's understanding, thereby informing instruction and next steps. Likewise, effective questioning plays a critical role in the work of a coach and the interaction between coach and teacher. What are some examples of effective coaching questions? What are the different ways that a coach might make use of questioning with a teacher? What purposes do different types of questions serve in coaching? It is this role of questioning that this chapter addresses through several different coaching cases.

Case: Different Questions for Different Purposes ∞ Nancy, Grade 1

In this case with a Grade 1 teacher, our discussion about her students' work with pattern blocks was structured by the questions I posed. These questions each had a specific purpose based on my coaching agenda that unfolded during the meeting.

SETTING THE STAGE

When I arrived at Nancy's first-grade classroom, she was seated at the back horseshoe table. Next to her I noticed a pile of her students' pattern block puzzle sheets from their work in the geometry unit. I was quite pleased to see that Nancy had taken my suggestion to have student work for us to look at together when we met; I had come with some general questions in mind to get us started, but I was all the more relieved when I saw that she had saved some student work for us to discuss together. It would be a good springboard for our conversation.

As we got started, Nancy moved the pile of work closer to me. She said, "This is what they just did the other day. They did pretty well. See, they filled in all the puzzles, and I had them write on the back . . . since we're supposed to make sure they're writing too, you know."

The student sheet (Figure 5.1) showed three identical pattern block fill-in puzzles. Children were to use the pattern blocks to find three different ways to fill in the puzzle. Her first graders had traced and colored the blocks they had used onto the page. As I looked through each page, I noticed that nearly every child had used a yellow hexagon pattern block in the middle of the pattern block puzzle. Although this was a very appropriate fill-in strategy, I found it interesting that so few of them had used a different combination of blocks for that center region as they filled in all three puzzles. I also noticed that on the back of the page each child had written a list of the blocks that he or she had used, obviously at the instruction of Nancy. For example, on the back of one sheet, a child had written, "I used 2 triangles. I used 3 diamonds. I used 1 hexagon."

MAKING THE MOVE: QUESTIONING TO GATHER DATA

With Nancy's comments and the student work in mind, I began to wonder what she understood about this pattern block activity and what her understandings were of the geometric ideas that the first-grade curriculum unit was intended to foster. I had some hunches that she saw this activity of filling in a design with shapes as a way for children to get to know the names of shapes. But I needed to learn more about what she was thinking.

KRW: It seems as if almost everybody used a hexagon block in the middle of the puzzle. What do you make of that?

Nancy: Yep. For some of them, though, it was really hard to see it was easiest to start with the largest block. Some of them saw it right away but for others I had to keep saying, "Look at the blocks. Which one do you think you should use first?" Finally, they all started to see that the hexagon fit there.

This gave me some more information about the manner in which the activity was undertaken and how Nancy perceived both the activity and her role as the teacher.

Figure 5.1 Pattern Block Student Sheet

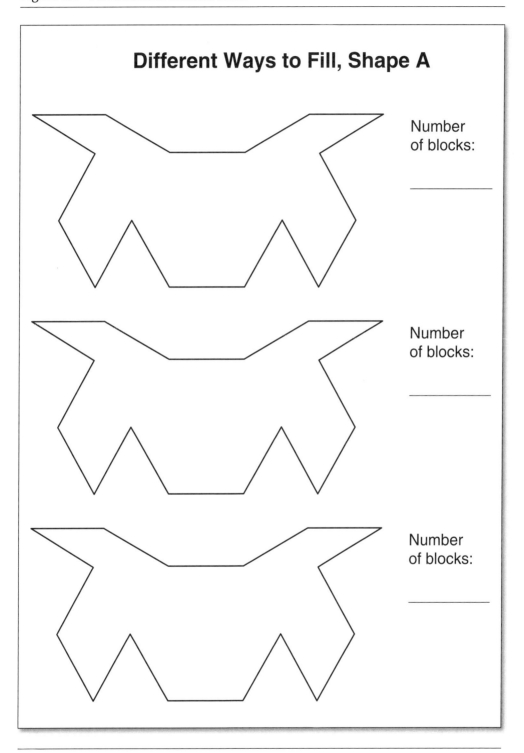

MAKING THE MOVE:
QUESTIONING TO UNCOVER THE MATH

I only had a half-hour for this conversation—I was already feeling pressed for time—so I decided to move the conversation at this point to the mathematics of the activity. I decided that I would draw our attention to the fact that all of the puzzles on the student sheet were the same and ask Nancy what she saw as the mathematics of the activity.

KRW: Now on this student sheet, all of the pattern block puzzles are the same. What do you see as the purpose of that?

Nancy: Well, it says that they needed to fill them in different ways.

KRW: Did they notice anything as they were filling them in different ways?

Nancy: It's funny. At the end, I had them share what blocks they used to fill in the puzzles and they all read what they wrote. They got all excited when they noticed that someone else used the same number of blocks as they did. But then they'd notice that the blocks were put in different places on the puzzle. They thought that was so neat!

KRW: Were there any who used different numbers of blocks?

Nancy: Oh, yeah, they started talking about that too (pointing to one student sheet on the table). Peter used five blocks here and then seven the second time. And then Kimberly used eight in one of hers. It was so funny how they were talking about all of that.

KRW: So they were noticing that they could use different shapes to fill the same space. That's a really important idea.

I wanted to push a little more here to uncover any other relationships the children may have explored, so I continued with another question.

KRW: Did they notice anything about the shapes when they were putting them together to fill the space?

Nancy thought for a moment. She did not have an immediate response and I noticed that I was just about to jump in with a new question. But then I reminded myself that wait time is as important when posing questions to teachers as it is when posing questions to students. A moment later, Nancy responded.

Nancy: Some of them were taking the blocks and saying that they could put two of the trapezoids together to make the hexagon block. And some put triangles on top of the trapezoids to show that too. But I don't think all of them really got that. Some of them just couldn't see it. I had to keep showing one boy how he was going out of the lines with blocks. He just couldn't see it.

At this point, I rephrased what Nancy had described to me about the powerful mathematical conversation that her first graders had had about how the different shapes could be put together to fill the same area (composing and decomposing space) and about the relationships of the different pattern blocks to one another. I pointed out to her that that student page was set up with identical puzzles for that very purpose of children exploring those ideas.

I had brought with me the second-grade geometry unit as well. I had learned from my meetings with other teachers that many of them did not have a sense of their grade-level unit in the context of what came before and what came after, so I thought perhaps the second-grade unit would be helpful to have with me when talking with Nancy. I decided to share with her how the second-grade geometry unit built on this work by exploring the relationships of the pattern blocks to one another more explicitly and asking children to predict how many of each block may cover a puzzle; in those predictions, children could draw on the relationships they had uncovered and continue to build their understandings of composing and decomposing space.

When I made this connection to the second-grade work, Nancy remarked, "Oh, I was at lunch the other day and had copied some of these pattern block puzzles, and Eleanor [a second-grade teacher in the building] said that she did those with her second graders. I thought for a minute that maybe I was doing the wrong unit, but now I see. They do it too, but it's different."

MAKING THE MOVE: QUESTIONING TO FOSTER NEXT STEPS

It was time for our conversation to come to a close for the day, but I wanted to leave Nancy with one more question to think about in connection with the mathematics of the pattern block puzzle activity and her students' work.

KRW: Since your children had that great conversation about filling the puzzle with different blocks, I wonder if more of them now might have other ways to fill in the middle that's different than just a hexagon.

I wondered if she was seeing how valuable it would be for students to fill that space with different combinations of blocks.

Nancy: Uh, well, . . . maybe I could do like a "before" and "after." I could give them this student sheet again and tell them they have to find a different way to fill in the middle.

TAKING A CLOSER LOOK

This coaching meeting with Nancy provides one snapshot of how questions posed in the moment might be used in a variety of ways, highlighting the different purposes of different questions and calling attention to the nature of the questions posed by a coach. Initially, I posed questions and listened closely to Nancy to gather information for myself about her level of understanding of the mathematics concepts and student thinking. This use of questioning—and listening—serves as a formative assessment tool that provides the coach with a sense of the pieces of mathematics or student work that might need to be examined more closely with the teacher.

After this initial data gathering and formulating a hunch as to the next step to take with Nancy based on that information, I then used a series of questions that were intended to push her reflection on the student work before us and the related activity in order to bring out the mathematical emphasis of the experience for students. At times, a single question such as "What's the math of this experience?" or "What do we want students to understand, know, and be able to do as a result of this experience?" can serve this purpose. In the case of Nancy, I instead used a series of questions grounded in the student work to probe her reflection on different aspects of the student work until at last we had constructed a full picture of what the mathematical ideas of the experience were. Framing these probing questions around the student work establishes neutral ground for the teacher-coach discussion and inquiry into student learning.

These coaching questions guide a teacher's reflection on practice and student learning. With that in mind, a final question in a coaching conference pushes the teacher to reflect on and consider the implications for practice: "What might you do next?" or "What would you do differently next time?" In the case of Nancy, you hear this prompt phrased not as a direct question but with the language of "I wonder . . . ." This, then, is not an outright question but rather is an implied question. I have found that presenting a prompt for reflection in this way models a reflective stance for the teacher and plants food for thought in a nonthreatening manner.

Although these questions were derived on the spot as the conversation unfolded with Nancy, they were not altogether spontaneous. They were guided by my overarching agenda for this teacher and the set of broad questions that can frame such an agenda. Not coincidentally, these questions parallel the critical coaching cycle elements described in Chapter 3:

- What's the math?
- What is the evidence of student learning that we see?
- What are the implications for practice and next steps?

In the moment, I need to shape how these questions are posed based on where the teacher is in his or her own development, and I also need to shape the questions based on the student work at hand. But the learning agenda that I keep in mind as a coach provides a scaffold for the questions I pose.

In other cases, particularly in a coaching cycle in which a debrief meeting follows a classroom visit later in the day or even the next day, a coach can prepare a series of more specific questions ahead of time to use to guide the conversation. For a beginning coach in particular, this can feel safer than the in-the-moment phrasing of questions. The case that follows shares insights into the thinking a coach undertakes when planning these questions for a coaching meeting.

Case: Planning the Questions ∞ Rick, Grade 4

This case presents the planning of questions that I undertook in preparation for a coaching conversation with a veteran Grade 4 teacher after observing a data lesson in his classroom. I had the opportunity to carefully craft and sequence the questions I would use in the meeting with the teacher, but it became evident quickly that even such a carefully formulated coaching plan needs to remain flexible to adjust to the teacher strategically in the moment.

SETTING THE STAGE

101, 97, 100, 104, 92, 108, 97, 95, 108, 91, 100, 111, 99, 108, 99, 96, 98, 101, 98

These were the raisin counts reported by the children in Rick's fourth-grade classroom as I sat in on the first session of their work in the data unit. Rick had given each student a snack-size box of raisins and asked for estimates of the number of raisins in the box. The children then counted the raisins in their boxes at their desks and came back together to report the counts. Rick recorded the counts on the dry erase board.

Rick: OK, good. We've got a lot of data here. It's really not very helpful the way I have it, so I'm going to have you find a way to organize and represent it. I have paper here you can use. You can work with a partner, and we'll use some groups of three if we need to.

As I circulated and observed the student work, two distinct variations of line plot representations for the raisin data seemed to emerge from the groups. In one, such as the line plot constructed by Shawn and Tori, every value from 91 to 111 was represented, even if no raisin counts of that value were reported. Some other groups, however, such as Paul and Adam, constructed a line plot that only represented the values of reported raisin counts; zero values were omitted from the line plot entirely.

```
                                                              X
                          X  X  X  X  X                       X
   X  X           X  X  X  X  X  X  X           X             X                  X
  90 91 92 93 94 95 96 97 98 99 100 101 102 103 104 105 106 107 108 109 110 111
```
A reconstruction of Shawn and Tori's line plot

```
                         X     X     X     X     X           X
   X     X     X     X   X     X     X     X     X     X      X     X
  91    92    95    96   97    98    99    100   101   104   108   111
```
A reconstruction of Paul and Adam's line plot

This seemed very interesting to me. What was it that made so many of the groups omit on their line plot any values for which there is no data, that is, values that have a frequency of zero? Then it occurred to me that in fact this probably fit with their prior understanding of zero. For so much of their mathematics work to date, zero had meant "nothing." This was not the case here, though. In the case of the line plots, zero does mean something in terms of the shape of the data. Including on the line plot the values for which there is no data shows the holes in the data and also makes the clumps of data more apparent. It seemed like a better sense of the distribution of the data across the range could be seen when the zero values were included in the line plot. I was interested in how students such as Paul and Adam might begin to think about that significance of zero in this work when they noticed the differences between their line plot and that of others in the class who had included the zero values.

In the whole-group sharing session, both Paul and Adam and Shawn and Tori shared their line plots. When Shawn and Tori shared their line plot, Rick asked them, "How is yours different from Paul and Adam's?" Shawn responded, "We have every number. Even if there wasn't anything there." Rick turned to the group and asked what they thought about that.

Jennifer responded, "I think the other one (Paul and Adam's) looks neater." A hum of agreement with this statement could be heard in the group. With that, Rick moved on to the reports of statements each group made before ending the session.

I was intrigued by what these students were thinking about the zero values. I wondered what Rick was thinking about all of this too and was eager to talk to him about it. As I waited for Rick to bring his students to their art class after the lesson, I collected my thoughts for our debriefing meeting.

MAKING THE MOVE:
QUESTIONING TO PUSH THE MATH

I decided that it might be helpful if we thought through the mathematics of the raisin data activity. As I noticed the different line plots students were producing, it reminded me why including values that have no data is critical in terms of an accurate shape of the data and making outliers evident. Clarifying the mathematics in this way had been important to me as I observed the children during the class session, so I knew pursuing it with Rick was important for accuracy of the mathematics for students. I also thought focusing on the mathematics would provide me with some important information about where Rick was in his understanding.

I jotted down a few questions that could prompt us to look at the mathematics in the raisin data activity:

- What's the math here?
- What were your goals?
- How would you describe the shape of the raisin data?

I also jotted down some questions about the line plots that Paul and Adam and Shawn and Tori had shared:

- What do you make of these two plots?
- What's different about them?
- Is that important? Why?

I thought talking about these specific pieces of student work could help ground the mathematics discussion and make the link to the classroom.

Rick and I had met earlier for a prelesson conversation, and I had asked him some questions about the mathematics of the lesson. He had mentioned some global goals of wanting his students to be able to read and interpret data in real-world situations. I had tried to push a bit further at the specifics of the mathematics in the raisin lesson but to no avail. I had decided to step back at that point and let the lesson unfold. Now that we had student thinking, conversations, and work to refer to, I hoped my questions could move him further into the mathematics in a nonthreatening way.

At our debrief meeting, Rick's first comment to me was a bit strong but not altogether surprising given the impression I had received at our earlier meeting. With his arms folded, he said, "So, now you get to tell me what I did wrong." Rather than engage in a defense of my work, I moved forward feeling confident with my decision to have crafted questions that focused on the student work. I was hopeful that this could be neutral ground for the conversation. I said to Rick, "Let's look instead at what your students did. Here's Shawn and Tori's line plot and here's Paul and Adam's line plot. What makes them different and does that matter mathematically?"

Our conversation never moved past that question. It was a rich question that kept Rick focused on the student work and allowed me to illustrate mathematical ideas related to outliers and the shape of data. Rick's initial resistant comment to me could have caught me off guard and put me on the defensive. I may have struggled to respond in a way that would have moved the coaching conversation forward. But, by jotting down questions ahead of time in preparation for this meeting, I could take a deep breath, look down at my notes, and pick the question that would keep the conversation on a more productive course.

TAKING A CLOSER LOOK

I knew I couldn't be certain how the meeting with Rick would unfold, but I felt more confident going into it with my notes and questions written as a framework for our discussion. As was the case with Nancy, my questions were framed according to an overarching learning agenda for the teacher:

- What's the math?
- What is the evidence of student learning that we see?
- What are the implications for practice and next steps?

But in the case with Rick, I could shape the questions ahead of time and sequence the questions carefully to build from the broad mathematics goals of the lesson to the specific pieces of student work that I had observed. Just as in the questions posed to Nancy, the questions for Rick would allow insights into his understanding and would then push him to develop deeper understanding of the mathematics, grounded in student work. In the moment, I needed to adjust, but that was possible because I had a framework that could guide my decision making.

It can be comforting as a coach to have the time to jot down a carefully thought-out sequence of well-phrased questions and come to a coaching meeting prepared with such questions. It is important to keep in mind, however, that even when these questions are written down ahead of time, they should be used as a guiding frame for the conversation, not as a rigid script to follow. The coach needs to listen carefully to the teacher's responses, remain flexible, and adjust the pacing and sequence of questions based on the teacher's responses and body language. Clearly, this was the case with Rick.

I can remember times when I sat at a coaching meeting locked into the questions that I had scripted ahead of time. If the teacher responded in a manner I was not expecting or brought another topic or issue to the table for discussion, I felt paralyzed and stumbled the rest of the way through the coaching conference. While a guiding agenda and a bank of carefully crafted coaching questions is extremely important as a coach, flexibility and an ability to recraft these questions in the moment to be responsive to the particular coaching situation remains essential.

In both Nancy's and Rick's cases, we see the use of generally open-ended, probing questions, grounded in student work. These are questions that highlight the role of the coach as a mediator between the mathematics, student learning, instructional practice, and teacher reflection. But before we bring the discussion of questioning to a close, let's turn to instances of more pointed, specific questions about teacher practice and the role those might play in coaching.

Case: When Open-Ended Questions Aren't Enough ∞ Carolyn, Grade 1

In my conversation with a first-grade teacher struggling with pacing of the district curriculum, I realized that offering short-term solutions, expressing empathy, or asking broad, open-ended questions would not get at the heart of the pacing issue. Instead, posing structured, precise questions prompted this teacher to reflect on and tease out for herself the specific causes of the pacing issue.

SETTING THE STAGE

I had not worked individually with Carolyn, a first-grade teacher in her fifth year of teaching in the district, but I had met her at the monthly first-grade math team meetings that were being held this year to support the implementation of a new standards-based curriculum. I was pleased when I received her e-mail asking if I would be willing to meet to help her with pacing. This pacing issue had come up at the team meetings as well, as all of the team members were struggling with this dimension of the implementation. Carolyn wanted to meet to talk about it further.

When I met with Carolyn and she shared that she was several weeks behind in pacing, I knew that she was hoping I would begin to offer suggestions as to how to compact lessons or omit certain experiences in the unit altogether for students. In the past, I think I had responded to pacing issues teachers raised in just that way because I wanted them to realize that I was hearing them and recognized their struggle. But this response never felt quite right, not only in terms of the impact on student learning but also in the sense that it never got at the heart of pacing issues. Certainly, we could compact lessons or omit some as a short-term fix that would bring a classroom back onto the pacing guide, but what was the underlying issue that had caused pacing to veer so far off course to begin with? How, as a coach, could I get at that with a teacher? I had been thinking about this the night before as I prepared for my meeting with Carolyn.

MAKING THE MOVE: QUESTIONING TO REFINE THE FOCUS

This time I didn't respond to Carolyn with a list of suggestions for compacting or omitting lessons. Instead, I responded with more questions.

KRW: OK, so let's try to tease out what it is that is so challenging in the pacing of the curriculum for you. . . . Is it that you're struggling with pacing within a lesson, meaning you look up at the clock and realize that you only have a few minutes left but are only halfway through the lesson; then it's taking you two days to get through one lesson?

My tone indicated that I had other aspects of pacing for her to think about before she answered. I paused to let her think for a moment about this first pacing scenario.

KRW: Or is it that you are struggling with pacing within the unit as a whole, meaning that after you teach a particular session, you are worried that some students have not mastered that concept, so rather than move on the next day, you are reteaching that same lesson.

Again I paused to let her consider this possibility.

KRW: Or is it that the lessons and unit are fine but you find that you keep including extra math activities that you have done in past years even though they aren't a part of this unit?

Of course, my hunch was that it was a bit of all of this, but if I could push Carolyn to isolate one that she felt was at the root of her pacing issues, then we would have a focus for her professional growth and potential coaching work together, much more so than if I simply listed lessons for her to compact.

Carolyn: Hmm. I think the biggest one for me is within a lesson. I know that the discussion at the end is important, but I'll look up and realize that time is up, that the kids have to go to lunch, and they've hardly had any time to work, let alone time to come back to meet to talk about it and share.

TAKING A CLOSER LOOK

Together we had identified a specific element of instructional practice to examine: pacing within a lesson. I mentioned to Carolyn that this is challenging because it requires that teachers head into a lesson being crystal clear about the mathematical goals they have for students that day. They have to be "tight" in terms of language and structure to keep the focus on how to develop that mathematical idea over the course of the math class time. Teachers also struggle with when to pursue (and when not to pursue) other tangential topics that students may bring up during a lesson launch or discussion, however mathematical those other topics may be. All of this comes to impact pacing within a lesson. For Carolyn, to dissect pacing was an experience that allowed her to reflect on practice in a new way.

This experience would not have been possible if I had only posed open-ended, invitational questions such as "How's the pacing going?" or "What might help with that?" There are many instances throughout the cases in this book in which global questions such as "What did you think of the lesson?"or "What did you notice?" are very effective in initiating dialogue between teacher and coach. They are nonthreatening, they communicate genuine respect for the teacher's perspective, and they allow the coach to gain insights into the teacher's thinking and concerns in order to inform the next coaching move.

But there are other times, such as with Carolyn, when more pointed, precise questioning must be used in order to probe deeper into an issue. Structured questions allow a coach to engage a teacher in peeling away the layers to reveal the underlying cause. Otherwise, coaching conversations may stay at a surface level, not pushing for the focused reflection and discussion that can allow the root of an issue to be surfaced and then tackled.

KEYS TO QUESTIONING

Regardless of the type or purpose of question being posed to a teacher, it is important to keep in mind the notion of wait time. It can be uncomfortable as a coach to put forth a question in a one-on-one conversation with a teacher and have silence follow. I can remember instances in which my concern for building a good relationship with a teacher would make the silence that followed a question all the more difficult. I worried that the silence was an indication that I was making the teacher uncomfortable, so I would jump in to "rescue" the teacher from the question. I would either answer it myself or pose a new question.

But then I realized that the silence can be an indicator of an effective coaching question. The silence following a coaching question most often means that a teacher is reflecting on the question and reflecting on practice. It means that the question posed was a thought-provoking question, one that has created a need to reflect or a sense of disequilibrium for the teacher. Disequilibrium might be uncomfortable but it is the hallmark of learning; in this case, being uncomfortable means that a teacher is in a space that is ripe for growth. It is the coach's role, then, to give wait time and actually push the teacher to feel uncomfortable. Now when I pose a question and there is wait time before the teacher responds, I know that I have posed a powerful question.

The scenarios of this chapter paint a picture of the different ways in which a coach may make use of questions. Whether it is formulating questions in the moment or preparing questions ahead of time, there are some guiding principles from the examples of Nancy, Rick, and Carolyn that can be valuable to keep in mind. They are shared below as yet more tools for the coach's toolbox.

Keys to Questioning

- **Develop coaching questions** that frame a learning agenda across three areas:

  1. The mathematics

  2. Student learning evidence (and instruction that supports that learning)

  3. Implications for practice and next steps

  (These areas parallel the critical elements for coaching conferences described in the Chapter 3 discussion of the coaching cycle.)

- **Use open-ended, invitational questions** such as "How do you think it went?" or "What did you notice?" to open the coaching conversation in a manner that shows interest in the teacher's perspective and conveys a sense of collaborative inquiry. Also, it provides the coach with valuable insights into the thinking of the teacher and potential points for further discussion.

- **Then be prepared to pose follow-up questions** that will ensure that the conversation becomes more specific and connected to evidence of student learning.

- **Develop a set of two or three powerful questions** that might push a teacher's reflection on his or her own practice after any lesson. By posing these questions to the teacher after each lesson (in a debrief meeting, over e-mail, etc.), the coach can help the teacher begin to internalize the questions and reflect on practice using these questions.

Examples: At what moment were students learning the most? And why was that?

Who was doing the most work or talking most in this lesson?

What was the most thought-provoking question you posed to students in the lesson? How did they respond?

- **Use more focused, structured questions** to probe an issue with greater specificity (i.e., pacing).
- **Use "I wonder..."** as language that implies a question but also suggests a collaborative tone of action research and inquiry between coach and teacher.
- **Be explicit with teachers that you are posing these questions purposely** as a coach to prompt their reflection on student learning and classroom practice. This can often alleviate some of the awkwardness that teachers may sense if they are new to coaching and hold an assumption that the coach will tell them what to do rather than raise questions to consider.
- **Practice, practice, practice.** Formulate questions you might ask in preparation for a coaching meeting (just as you would write a lesson plan as a classroom teacher). Write questions ahead of time on an index card and bring this with you as a reference during a coaching meeting.
- **Remain flexible in questioning.** Prepare ahead of time, but be ready to adjust in the moment of coaching.
- **Use wait time liberally.** Don't rush in to rescue the teacher. The silence that follows a question you pose can mean that the teacher is reflecting on practice or has been pushed to a point of disequilibrium; this means the question was a powerful one.

Questions for Reflecting and Linking to Practice

1. Consider examples of questions you might use in coaching encounters with teachers. How would you describe the purpose that each of these questions serves in terms of moving forward the learning agenda that you have for a teacher?

2. In the case of Carolyn, structured questions were used to peel away the layers of a pacing issue. What other situations or issues might lend themselves to such focused, structured questioning by the coach?

3. What techniques or strategies might help you cope with silence or challenging responses when posing questions to teachers?

6

Being Explicit

Carefully crafted, purposeful questions, such as those examined in the previous chapter, can prompt teacher reflection on practice and student learning. But are there instances in which these questions seem to be limited in the steering of a coaching conversation or in moving a teacher to a new level of understanding? Might there be perspectives, knowledge, or skill sets that must be shared explicitly by the coach so that they can then be applied, practiced, and truly owned by the teacher? Although probing questions are clearly a powerful and effective component of the coach's toolbox, some situations do seem to require a more direct approach or communication of perspectives or knowledge from coach to teacher. I liken this to the balance that is important in an inquiry-based classroom, a balance the teacher achieves between open-ended questioning techniques and more explicit, direct instruction when there is knowledge or information that students need to move forward with their learning. This chapter presents a case of "being explicit" so that we can hear examples of this type of coaching move and consider how to find a balance of moves as a coach.

Case: Making Explicit Moves ∞ Keith, Grade 4

As I observed this Grade 4 teacher at work in math class over a period of several weeks, I became increasingly concerned about the lack of engagement of students and the need for more "time on math" for students. I needed to expand my repertoire of coaching moves beyond invitational moves to those that were more direct and explicit.

SETTING THE STAGE

Keith was a fourth-grade teacher in his sixth year of teaching in our district. I was working with Keith as part of an eight-week rotation of coaching experiences for teachers at his grade level and was hopeful for a powerful, collaborative experience. Keith and I had worked together on summer curriculum projects, and in that work, I heard him express his growing understanding of the student thinking that could be developed in mathematics classrooms using a standards-based program. I also knew that he had a sincere interest in and comfort level with the mathematics content of the fourth-grade curriculum.

When I first met with Keith to define our coaching work for the next eight weeks, he was more than willing to commit to planning meetings once each week. He was very comfortable with classroom visits, observations, and coteaching sessions several times each week in his math class, and he was open to spending additional time together as needed to reflect on past lessons or student work in debrief meetings. He seemed committed to the coaching cycle, and I was excited at the possibility of using this coaching experience to support Keith in crafting truly effective instruction that would bring together mathematical content and deep understanding of student learning. But after four weeks of classroom visits, I was not feeling satisfied with our work together.

FRAMING THE DILEMMA

What I saw each time I arrived in Keith's classroom were 22 students sitting at desks arranged in groups of 5 or 6, with Keith standing at the overhead projector in the front of the room. Keith had an easy-going, very personable style with his students; they enjoyed his references to his family and stories of his own school experience. Keith felt quite at ease with the mathematical content of the curriculum; he used his computation strengths to make solutions appear effortless in front of his students, and he shared with them the real-world connections that made mathematics relevant and meaningful. In all of this, though, I watched as students sat back to listen to Keith each day in class. Some students offered their own thoughts and connections, and Keith was quick to bring those students into a conversation with him. Other students sat as passive observers of the class or fidgeted with pens, pencils, and the like at their desks. The nature of the dialogue was teacher-to-student-to-teacher, all well intended and focused on making the mathematical content interesting, but I found myself wondering what meaning students were making for themselves.

I attempted to use questioning techniques at our meetings to push Keith's reflections on his math class sessions. I asked questions such as "What evidence of student learning did you see in class today?" or "What might you do differently next time?" Each time, Keith's answers suggested that he was quite satisfied with his instructional practice. He spoke with such general statements as "I think it went well" or "I think they really got it." I was searching for the piece of student work or excerpt of dialogue from the classroom that would bring our discussions to a level of greater specificity in terms of the mathematics and student learning.

Keith did express frustration with the constant need he saw to reteach and revisit previously taught concepts because students did not seem to hold onto them. I used this as an entry point to probe further with questions such as "What can we do to develop more robust student learning for these concepts?" and "How will we know if students are truly learning what you intend them to learn?" Keith saw the information he presented to students in the whole-group structure as the critical element, and if students continued to struggle with a concept, he spoke of the need for reteaching in the sense of reviewing the ideas in the whole-group lecture format before moving forward with the unit. My questions and Keith's reflections were not generating any sense of urgency for change. I was becoming more and more frustrated as I realized how few opportunities we had to talk about fostering student learning since the classroom structure was not allowing students' mathematical ideas to be visible.

COLLECTING DATA

I sat as an observer for one 50-minute class period as Keith spoke with the students about units of liquid measure and their relationships to one another. He engaged some of the students in the discussion by referencing water bottles that they had on their desks. Others, however, seemed disconnected. I took note of the time, wondering if perhaps data related to the pacing of the class session components might be useful in my later meeting with Keith about the lesson. The class began at 9:05 AM; at 9:40 AM, I recorded the time and, noting that Keith was still discussing ideas to the whole group, I stepped forward. My movement caught Keith's eye and he paused.

Keith: Mrs. Woleck, would you like to add something to our discussion?

KRW: Sure. Since you've shared so many different ideas about liquid measure, maybe it would be helpful for everyone to try to use these ideas now to tackle some problems about measurement.

Keith had collected a variety of real-world liquid measurement scenarios (recipes, beverages for sporting events, etc.) that students were to work on in pairs; he and I had discussed these tasks at our earlier prelesson conference. With this nudge from me, he agreed and grouped the students with partners for all to begin that work. I recorded the time: 9:45 AM. There was a buzz in the room as students began working on their tasks, and there was much student conversation about the comparison and application of measurement units. At 9:50 AM, Keith announced the homework assignment as the group put their materials away to prepare to move to art class. Math class was over.

MAKING ONE MOVE

I gathered my notes for the debrief conversation with Keith. I wondered if he realized the engagement with mathematical ideas that occurred during those final minutes of the math class. I began our meeting with a question crafted to move the conversation toward student learning and the power of the period of student interaction and dialogue. I asked, "At what point in today's class did you think students were learning the most?"

I fully expected Keith to cite the last five minutes of the class with students engaged in discussing and applying measurement understandings to the problem-solving tasks. To my surprise, he did not reference that segment of the class at all. Instead, he mentioned the class segment in which he introduced a graphic organizer to help students remember the relationship between cups, pints, quarts, and gallons.

My mind began racing as I considered my next move with Keith. I knew that I could certainly validate his comment and we could discuss the value of graphic organizers and representations in mathematics class, particularly for visual learners. However, I didn't see that as a move that would push Keith's practice to a new level, and I didn't feel that move would lead to deeper student understanding. I realized that he did not recognize the importance of student dialogue in constructing mathematical ideas and understandings and that my probing questions were not serving as a vehicle for getting at this critical piece of practice. I realized that I needed to challenge his thinking about this more directly.

MAKING A SECOND, MORE EXPLICIT MOVE

I felt myself getting nervous. I knew that I needed to be explicit about what I was seeing—and not seeing—in the math class, but I also knew that it was never easy for me to do this with a teacher. Why, though, was this so hard, so uncomfortable for me as a coach? I often challenge teachers' thinking and practice in professional development workshops and seminars; I don't feel the hesitancy there. I think the difference is that the one-on-one structure of a coaching meeting creates an intimacy that is much different than in a group meeting or workshop setting. When an explicit, direct statement—particularly one that challenges or raises questions about a teacher's practice—is put forth in a coaching meeting, there is no buffer between the coach and the teacher. And however the teacher responds, the full intensity of it is felt by the coach; there are no others in the room who might deflect it.

It is a risk on the part of the coach. But I knew that without this risk, our work would remain stalled. So I took a deep breath and spoke to Keith.

KRW: Every time I see you in class, I see you working very hard. You have a great relationship with your students. You enjoy the math. But *you* are the one doing all the work. What we want is to see the students doing more of the work like when they worked with their partner on the measurement problems you gave them; they were talking and really thinking hard about how liquid measures are related. But that was only the last five minutes of the class.

I paused and waited for Keith to respond. He sat looking thoughtful for what was only a few seconds but what felt much longer to me. I reminded myself about wait time. Then Keith agreed.

Keith: They did do some good work in those last five minutes. I didn't mean for the introduction to go on for so long.

KRW: So let's look at how to get them to that work sooner in the class. It's just a quick launch, maybe 5 or 10 minutes, at the beginning of class, and then send them off to get working with the ideas. You can always bring them back together later if you need to.

Keith: Right.

But as our conversation came to a close, I wasn't sure how he was processing this conversation and what impact it might really have on his practice. I had been explicit, but had I said too much? This balance felt very tricky.

THE NEXT VISIT

When I returned to a math class in Keith's room the following week, I was thrilled to see him offer just a five-minute introduction to a set of algebraic thinking and reasoning problems that were new to students. We had discussed this in our planning session, but I still worried that he might fall back to his ways of describing extensively the work to students and spending the majority of the time demonstrating multiple examples to the class as a whole. I was relieved to see that he held to our plan of a brief launch. He then moved students into groups of four to discuss a set of these problems together. As another part of our planning meeting, Keith and I had discussed how small groups may be an instructional strategy that would bring more students actively into the mathematics work of a lesson and allow them to develop understanding collaboratively. He had used small groups in language arts lessons and was willing to try it in this math lesson as well.

Keith and I circulated among the groups as they worked. The power of the student thinking as they shared their strategies for solving the problems and the reasoning they used was exciting. I couldn't wait to talk with Keith about the lesson after class. Would he recognize the difference in the student engagement, interaction, and discourse? What would he attribute this to?

I came to the postlesson meeting prepared with some probing questions to lead Keith through the debrief, but before I posed any of them, he began the conversation.

Keith: I've been thinking a lot about our conversation after the last class visit you made and again at our planning meeting. About making the introductions shorter. About getting students to do the work more and to work in groups. I've been trying that the past few days.

Our conversation continued a bit more about the student groups and the reasoning we heard the students using in their discourse with one another in the small groups. I wanted our conversation to validate the risk Keith took in this lesson; highlighting our observations of the student discourse and student learning did just that. At the end of the meeting, it was Keith who had a question to ask:

Keith: But what I'm not sure about is how I would do this if you weren't in the classroom. With two of us, we could get around to all the groups, but what about when I'm by myself here?

He was asking the difficult questions. These were the questions that could focus and propel our work together. As unsettling as it might have felt for Keith when he realized these were the questions he needed to confront in his practice, it felt much more satisfying as a coach to reach this point.

CONTINUING THE WORK TOGETHER

As I continued to coach Keith for the next few weeks, our conversations moved to a new depth and there was a true investment in the work from him. Not only did we meet each week, but between meetings, we would e-mail back and forth as he processed his ideas for his lessons. Some of this professional dialogue focused on group dynamics and classroom culture, but more and more, our conversations—both face-to-face and online—shifted to the mathematics of the lessons, for now the math was becoming more visible to him in the student thinking and dialogue that was occurring in the classroom.

In those next weeks, Keith worked to develop classroom structures that would support partner and group work in his classroom. He implemented some lessons that were perhaps too open-ended and afforded too little focus to students, but he then worked to refine these lessons to find the most effective guiding questions for students or the balance of structure that would best support the students in constructing meaning and uncovering mathematical relationships for themselves. Now Keith was searching for that balance in his own teaching that I had been seeking in my work with him as a coach.

TAKING A CLOSER LOOK

In their book, *Content-Focused Coaching: Transforming Mathematics Lessons*, Lucy West and Fritz Staub (2003) describe two kinds of coaching moves: (1) those that invite teacher contributions and (2) those that provide the teacher with direct assistance in designing mathematics lessons (see the following boxed text).

Two Kinds of Coaching Moves

- Moves that invite teacher contributions: "Statements or questions by the coach that initiate and invite the teacher to verbalize perceptions, thoughts, plans, deliberations, and arguments."
- Moves that provide direct assistance with lesson design: "Statements by the coach that provide guidance and explanations for specific designs and ways of implementing a lesson."

Source: From West & Staub (2003), p. 15.

West and Staub (2003) assert that for coaching to be effective in promoting growth in teacher practice, coaches need to keep a balance between invitational moves and moves of direct assistance. This also suggests that there are different stances that a coach may take when working with a teacher. That is, coaches may take on the stance of a collaborator when planning together or coteaching in the classroom. They may take on a stance of mediator between practice and reflection when posing questions in a postconference. And when offering more direct, explicit assistance to a teacher, the coach is stepping into a stance that parallels that of a consultant.

In my first years as a coach, I would find myself talking too much in my coaching meetings with teachers. Offering direct assistance and explanations like a consultant felt easy, as I assumed that by sharing what worked in my practice, teachers would adopt these practices in their own classrooms. I soon realized that, although a teacher would nod as I spoke and perhaps even try to implement a suggestion I offered, rarely did substantive change occur for that teacher because she had no opportunity to shape the idea for herself. The teacher was simply doing what I told her to do. I think in many cases these were easy conversations for the teachers as well because they only needed to listen and "do." My stance was leaning too heavily toward consultant, describing to teachers ways to implement lessons.

I then began to focus my coaching work on posing the right question at the right time and was quite pleased at my growth in this dimension of coaching. I began to use questioning as my primary coaching tool. But then I began to encounter situations such as my work with Keith that pushed me to realize that questions alone may at times limit the work. I was relying almost exclusively on invitational moves intended to prompt teacher reflection; often these were very effective moves, but there was still a balance that was missing and it resulted in prolonged work with teachers that seemed to be stalled and flat for both of us.

While I continue to find myself much more comfortable with moves that entail crafting and posing questions to teachers that prompt their reflection on practice and student learning, I also recognize that there is a time for being explicit and direct. Being explicit and direct in the sense of explaining a lesson design as West and Staub (2003) outline or offering an instructional strategy in a consultant stance is one example. But there seems to be another dimension of being explicit that entails calling the teacher's attention to the reality of what is happening in the classroom.

In the case of my work with Keith, being explicit and direct meant first pushing him to confront what Collins (2001) would call the "brutal facts," the reality of what was occurring in his classroom (p. 65). This use of an explicit move challenges directly the student learning that is occurring in the classroom as well as the teacher's beliefs about effective practice. Such explicit moves are much harder to initiate and navigate in a manner that is respectful of teachers' practice and belief systems, but they give a balance of tools to the coach to ensure that a learning agenda moves forward for the teacher.

Why Be Explicit?

Explicit moves made by a coach can serve two purposes:

1. To push a teacher to confront the realities of student learning in the classroom from a different lens or perspective, particularly when questioning techniques seem to be ineffective and mathematics learning is being compromised in the classroom for students

2. To suggest or share new instructional strategies, techniques, or practices not presently in a teacher's repertoire or not currently being used in the classroom by the teacher

Often, one purpose leads to the other; that is, as a teacher recognizes that current practices are not resulting in student learning, there is often an opening for suggesting and then examining alternate practices or strategies collaboratively.

KEYS TO BEING EXPLICIT

As I look back on the experience with Keith and consider the moment of being explicit—that moment of pushing him to see who was really doing all of the work in the class—I realize that there were elements of the coaching situation that rendered that direct move effective. As hard as it was even then for me to abandon reflective questioning moves for the moment and switch to a more direct approach, Keith and I had already developed a professional relationship grounded in trust and mutual respect. Prior to this class session, I had spent several weeks in his class-room and met with him, and we had had many informal opportunities over the year to get to know each other at grade-level meetings and through curriculum projects. I knew that he welcomed honest feedback and that he both respected and trusted me as a coach. I was frustrated that so much time had passed in our work without getting to this point of moving forward, but that time was necessary for us to build the rela-tionship that allowed me to be explicit and challenge him to take a risk in his teaching. This speaks to the importance of coaching as an ongoing experience with a teacher, not as an isolated meeting or single visit to a classroom.

Also important is the coach's tone in instances of being explicit. My tone with Keith was matter-of-fact and I was able to reference specific evi-dence and data related to students and practice in the classroom. When I stated my concern and raised urgency for change, I referenced the power of those final five minutes of the math class. Taking specific notes, as detailed as the time of transitions in the classrooms, gave me objective data to call upon in the conversation. Keith interpreted my direct approach not as an attack on his practice but rather as constructive feedback grounded in the shared purpose of student learning.

After making that explicit, direct move with Keith at our meeting, I left feeling satisfied that we had talked candidly about the issue. I felt I had been explicit while maintaining the collaborative nature of our conversa-tion. Still, I did not expect to walk into Keith's classroom the following week and see anything different. I knew I had put forth an important idea for him to think about but I believed it would take several more sessions and conversations together to examine the idea further and move him to a place of "having a go" with it in his classroom.

What supported Keith in moving forward with this work on his own? I believe it was in part due to the fact that Keith knew that our work was ongoing and that I would return that following week to continue our coaching work together. I sent brief e-mails in the time between the visits to confirm our meeting time but also to casually note some lingering thoughts I had and to inquire as to whether he had other thoughts. There was an implicit message that all of this was still in progress and that we would each be thinking about it in the time between our visits.

It was one of those wonderful moments as a coach to walk into the classroom that next week and witness the manner in which Keith had processed the conversation. It was even more powerful to listen to him raise his own questions and feel comfortable enough to share with me his own fears related to this work. I won't pretend that all instances of being explicit work out as nicely.

Three Factors That Enhance the Effectiveness of an Explicit Move

- A trusting relationship must be well established between the teacher and coach. This is not determined merely by the length of time the coach and teacher have worked together; trust or openness to explicit moves may come quickly if the coach is perceived to be highly competent in the eyes of the teacher.
- The explicit move must be framed in evidence of student learning, such as scripts from the classroom, a student work sample, or assessment data, to provide a third-point reference.
- Follow-up support from the coach in continuing to examine and reflect upon the issue must be possible, eminent, and anticipated.

Questions for Reflecting and Linking to Practice

1. What other moves might you have considered in the situation with Keith? Which of these are "invitational" and which are examples of being explicit? How would you make a decision as to which of the many possible moves to use with Keith?

2. Describe a situation you have encountered in which the coaching conversations and use of reflective questions have stalled. What might be the reasons for this and what explicit moves might you consider to reignite the coaching and learning agenda for the teacher?

3. What cautions must a coach keep in mind when choosing to be explicit in the work with a teacher?

7

Using Data

Data has become an integral part of the work in schools. Data-based decision making is used in districts to ensure that school improvement plans are focused and to target student learning goals. Standards-based education, accountability through state testing, and federal legislation have resulted in more data than ever being digested by schools as they seek to determine their next steps. This focus is not only on data at the district or school level but also on data at the level of the classroom and individual student. Policy initiatives such as Response to Intervention (RTI) and the calls for differentiation and responsive teaching in classrooms to meet the needs of struggling students and the range of learners have resulted in teachers analyzing their own student data more than ever to inform instructional decisions.

What does all of this mean for the coach? Just as curriculum materials can be harnessed to foster teacher growth and impact student learning, how can the wealth of available student data in a district be used by coaches in their work with teachers? Moreover, how can data be used to gauge the impact of the coach's work and ultimately demonstrate the efficacy of coaching? This chapter will present a coaching case focused on a teacher's unexpected reaction to data and will then examine the tools that a coach can use when structuring coaching work around student data.

Case: Creating Urgency Through Data ∽ Peggy, Grade 5

In this case, my meeting with a Grade 5 teacher focused on her students' recent state testing performance data. When I observed the teacher's reaction to the data, I needed to reframe her analysis of the data in a manner that would not allow for excuses but would also not leave her paralyzed by her sense of failure. I needed to reframe the analysis in a manner that would create a sense of urgency as well as efficacy on her part in terms of growing her practice.

SETTING THE STAGE

As I arrived at Peggy's classroom for our September coaching meeting to discuss her student testing data, I did not anticipate any surprises. For the third year in a row, all Grade 5 teachers had been provided with the spring state testing data for those students they had taught in the previous year as well as those students that they would be teaching in this year ahead. They were all familiar with the set of guiding questions I sent with the scores to focus their analysis of and reflection on the data. They were always eager to see the results of their past year's students. At team meetings in September, they would talk with each other about what strategies they had used to develop student competency in the various strands of the test. They often used the data to select strands that they wanted to work on in the year ahead as a grade level.

I expected to hear many of the same responses from Peggy that I had heard from teachers in past years. With that in mind, I was determined going into the meeting not to allow Peggy to find excuses for poor student performance, excuses such as the home environment or emotional issues of a student. I felt that if we were truly going to move forward with practice and responding to the needs of all students, then we needed to own the data results and not dismiss any to factors that were beyond our control. I would need to state that explicitly but matter-of-factly if I heard "excuses" in response to the data.

I had been working with Peggy for three years; while we had built a friendly relationship over these years, I was not satisfied with the growth in her classroom over this period. I was determined to push her further this year. I knew that to move forward I was going to need to be firm if she put forth excuses for the poor student performance at our meeting. I was all the more shocked then when I heard the response from Peggy just minutes after I arrived. Peggy said, "I was really surprised when I saw this data. . . . I feel like such an awful teacher. They did horribly."

Her body language demonstrated to me that these were feelings of sincere remorse and disappointment. I too had noted in my review of the data that students in her class performed poorly compared to the school population as a whole. But I didn't want to jump in with my analysis; I wanted Peggy to unpack the data and come to conclusions for herself. I asked her to say more about what she was finding in the data. She replied, "I just thought they had come further than this. I feel like I failed them last year."

MAKING THE MOVE

At this point, I realized I was at a very delicate point with Peggy. I found myself tempted to jump in with excuses for her, such as the struggles some of these students had had even in fourth grade or the learning issues that impacted some of them. But then I realized that this would actually give Peggy permission to make excuses for her students' performance. This was exactly what I had wanted to avoid in this data analysis. Yet, her response here worried me because I didn't want her to simply throw her hands up in defeat. I knew that how I took the next steps with her would be critical in terms of finding a balance between owning student performance data and not feeling paralyzed.

I probed a bit more.

KRW: What evidence did you have from the classroom that makes this data so surprising to you?

Peggy: On all of the trimester tests, they could do everything. Maybe not perfectly, but they could do it. Or at least I thought they could.

She still was not speaking with the specificity or detail that would support deep analysis of the data, so I suggested that we look at some specific strands of the testing data. This allowed her to see those strands in which students had performed well and then consider the strands that were weak. In several cases, she was surprised by the weak strands. One approach would have been to unpack those particular strands further and have Peggy focus on her instruction relative to the mathematics those strands entailed, but I felt that there was another issue that needed to be put on the table. I needed to push Peggy to reflect on her instructional practice specifically, yet I also needed to tread carefully given her strong reaction to the data.

SHIFTING THE CONVERSATION

I decided then that it might be useful to reframe the data analysis for Peggy. I needed her to shift to a more generative approach rather than feeling overwhelmed by the disappointing performance results. I also wanted to ensure that she didn't see this data as a call to drill students on the range of isolated strands in hopes that this would improve results for her current students. I needed to find a way to leverage this data to create a willingness on Peggy's part to examine instructional strategies she used in the classroom.

KRW: Since you are so surprised by the data, it might be important to consider generating some hypotheses about why it was so surprising. Because, really, test data shouldn't surprise us; it might not always be the data we want to see, but it shouldn't surprise us if we've been monitoring progress in an ongoing way. One question we can ask is how was the testing situation different from the classroom setting? How were students prepared to demonstrate their learning in both of those settings?

Peggy paused for a moment and I let her sit with those questions. Then she replied.

Peggy: I guess maybe I was helping them to answer questions more than I thought I was. So then on the test they couldn't do it themselves.

This was exactly what I believed was at the heart of the issue for Peggy. She would scaffold experiences for students and offer so many accommodations in the classroom that it distorted the ongoing assessment data she gathered. What's more, she had insisted on whole-group instruction throughout the year because she insisted it was working for her students. Now with this data, we could begin to rethink how instruction could be approached in her classroom together, not because I urged her to but because the data were telling her that her students needed her to.

TAKING A CLOSER LOOK

The case of Peggy illustrates the manner in which data can be used to create a sense of urgency not simply at a district or school level, but also at the level of the individual teacher. What is it about data that makes them so powerful? Data are objective. Whereas coaching conversations may fall flat when a teacher insists that a given practice has worked for years, data bring to the conversation snapshots of reality that cannot easily be ignored. Data are also student focused. These are the students that teachers and coaches share. If the performance of past students is weak, then there is urgency to determine what must occur to avoid such results for another group of students. Data allow students to be the springboard for conversation.

There is a delicate balance to be had here, however. Examining the data of students is poignant, and in some cases this can be painfully personal for the teacher. When the data show student growth, teachers can celebrate that their long hours of work and commitment have made a difference for a child. But when the data do not show growth, teachers may question all that they had so firmly believed was "good" teaching; this realization can be overwhelming for some teachers, but if guided by a coach, it can lead to the sense of urgency that brings with it a willingness to engage in reflection and change. This was the delicate balance that was needed with Peggy.

Without the thoughtful, careful steering by the coach, Peggy may have simply put away the data because they were too painful for her to confront or she may have felt helpless and paralyzed by the data. Reframing the data analysis process to ensure she was generating hypotheses that would prompt reflection and spur a sense of efficacy in terms of moving forward with her practice was essential work by the coach.

TOOLS TO FACILITATE THE USE OF DATA

For teachers to engage in data conversations with a coach, they first must have data in a form that is readable and usable. In most districts, this data will include statewide testing data and so it becomes important to consider the format that is used to report this data to classroom teachers. If a school receives its testing data as alphabetical listings of all students at a given grade, it is essential that the data are sorted by class so that teachers do not need to sift through pages of data to find their students. In cases in which the data do not arrive until the following school year, it is important to sort the data first for teachers to examine the performance of students they taught in the previous year and to then share data sorted by class for the upcoming school year. Examination of the performance of students from the previous year prompts teacher reflection on their curricular imple- mentation and instructional practices. Examination of data related to incoming students allows teachers to plan proactively for the strengths and needs of their new students. Looking back and looking forward can both be powerful professional development experiences through data.

The data must also be meaningful data. A composite score, for instance, may give a global sense of a student's mathematical proficiency, but it may not be useful data to analyze for targeted instruction. Analyzing data at the strand level—such as number, operations, and measurement, or even at a more specific level as place value, counting, and equivalent fractions—requires that more data are organized, but it can result in more focused conversations about student mathematical needs. Districts are, of course, at the mercy of educational testing companies in terms of the strand-level data that are released, but district assessment data can be pur- posely recorded and organized to allow for this level of analysis. For instance, district assessment items can be aligned to state standards or strands. A spreadsheet can then be developed for recording item-by-item performance for each student (Figure 7.1). This spreadsheet allows a teacher to undertake item analysis of the data, looking for trends at the class level and at the level of the individual student.

A full discussion of assessment data is beyond the scope of this book, but it should be noted that a balance of both qualitative and quantitative data is needed to paint a full picture of a student and to determine student strengths and needs. For this reason, I define data here to include both quantitative and qualitative data. Qualitative data could include student work on constructed-response test items or simply a set of student work

Figure 7.1 District Assessment Data Spreadsheet by Strand

Grade 3 Fall Checkpoint																									
	1. Place Value				2. Pictorial Rep of Numbers			4. Order, Magnitude, and Rounding	5. Models for Operations				6. Basic Facts		9. Solve Word Problems		10. Numeric Estimation Problems	11. Estimating Solutions	19. Tables, Charts, and Graphs			21. Probability	22. Patterns		24. Classification and Logical Reasoning	25. Math Applications
Name	1	2	3	4	5	6	7	8	9	10	11	12	13	14	15	16	17	18	19	20	21	22	23	24	25	0,1,2,3
1																										
2																										
3																										
4																										
5																										
6																										
7																										
8																										
9																										
10																										
11																										
12																										
13																										
14																										
15																										
16																										
17																										
18																										
19																										
20																										

Source: New Canaan Public Schools, New Canaan, Connecticut.

produced during a classroom lesson. Protocols can be used to ensure close analysis of the student work. In the case of formal performance-based assessments in a district, anchor sets should be available to communicate expectations for proficiency and quality of work. Unit checklists or other systems for recording anecdotal observations in the classroom, particularly in the case of young children, can also provide windows into student learning and points of reference when triangulating multiple sources of data. For some teachers, they will need the guidance of a coach to develop systems for recording qualitative data in the classroom and to support the close examination of work samples.

As a coach meets with a teacher to examine data, it can be helpful to present a set of guiding questions to frame the analysis and reflection. This can prevent a teacher from being overwhelmed by the data and can provide an entry point into the analysis. These should be questions that structure the manner in which a teacher examines the data; they should bring the teacher further and further into the data. The questions are intended to prompt reflection on the part of the teacher and also should allow teachers to begin to generate their own questions and hypotheses based on the data. The guiding data questions I used with Peggy and her colleagues at data meetings are provided in Figure 7.2.

DEVELOPING STUDENT-FOCUSED ACTION PLANS

While the organization and examination of data is important, the critical piece of work for a coach entails pushing a teacher to consider the implications of the data on teaching and learning in the classroom. This requires pushing beyond descriptive analysis of data to ask the question "So what?" to generate focused action plans that will impact instructional practice and student learning. This is not to say that the descriptive analysis, using a set of guiding questions, should be rushed or overlooked; indeed, taking time to thoroughly understand the data and raise questions and hypotheses ensures that the so-what actions are thoughtful, grounded in data, and targeted. Skipping thorough analysis to jump prematurely to action will only result in narrowly defined and perhaps short-sighted quick fixes that may or may not address the root cause of a student's or group's poor performance.

At the same time, some teachers can spend hours analyzing data but then file this data away in a folder or filing cabinet; instruction in the classroom continues for all as it had before. This then negates the potential impact of the data analysis. It is here where the coach's role is critical. Coaching conversations about data can shift from analysis to the development of action plans. These may be action plans that address a specific aspect of instructional practice for the entire class. For instance, one teacher

Figure 7.2   Guiding Questions for Data Analysis

Examine the data from several perspectives: *grade level, class, and individual student.*

- What **strengths** are evident in the data?

- What areas are **in need of support?** Identify one to three strands.

- What **surprises** you about the data?

- What **curriculum components** or **instructional practices** may be attributed to the strengths that are evident?

- What might we examine in curriculum or institutional practices to **address areas in need of support?**

- How can you use this data to improve classroom instruction for your students?

- What **other information or data** might be valuable to you in analyzing these results with regard to student learning and implications for instruction?

- Other comments, observations, etc.?

realized that while data on learning basic facts for her class was strong, class performance in the word problems strand was weak; with the coach, she developed an action plan to embed basic facts and computation work into more applied story problems to provide students with more instructional experiences in that area.

Action plans may also be designed to target specific students; these in fact have been some of the most powerful action plans that I have developed with teachers. Given the data profile of a particular student, an action plan is developed to address the targeted area of weakness. This action plan includes a statement of the specific goal for the student—a specific, measurable goal related to a particular concept, skill, or understanding, rather than a broad goal of "improving math." It also includes a small set of instructional experiences that can support this goal for the student; these experiences are to be facilitated by the teacher in guided math groups or one-on-one conferencing with the student during math class, with other students engaged in independent, pair, or small-group work appropriate to their needs or the given curriculum unit. In an RTI model, this becomes one vehicle for providing intervention—small-group, supplemental support—in the context of the classroom.

Perhaps the most vital component of the student-focused action plan is the action log that is kept in the classroom. This action log notes the goal and provides a place for the teacher to record each focused intervention session undertaken with the student (Figure 7.3). The action log allows the frequency and fidelity of the intervention implementation to be visible, but more important, it serves as a point of reference for future coaching meetings to discuss student progress toward the goal. I have called these meetings "student progress monitoring" meetings with teachers to distinguish them from coaching meetings in which we are looking at a particular lesson or curriculum unit. Our focus is on the student and evidence of growth, but the conversations naturally lead to discussion of what it takes to structure a mathematics classroom to allow for such small-group or individual conferencing to happen to address a student's particular needs.

Teachers are typically more than eager to meet to talk about their specific student needs; there is a shared purpose in our focus on the student. A coach can approach the more threatening conversations about practice, classroom structures, and curriculum implementation during these progress-monitoring meetings through the discussion of meeting the needs of a specific student. It is coaching, but it is coaching through students.

KEYS TO USING DATA

Getting to this point of "coaching through students" is dependent on prework that renders data accessible and meaningful. Throughout this chapter, I have noted what this prework entails in terms of sorting data by

Figure 7.3   Student-Focused Action Log

MATHEMATICS ACTION LOG

Name of student: _____   Classroom teacher: _____

Student learning goal/objective:

Suggested instructional strategies/resources:

Action log/progress notes:

Date	Focus of Instruction/ Learning Experience	Notes/Next Steps
	Make a copy and give to math coach	

teacher (both previous-year student data and upcoming-year data), developing district assessment templates that support focused data analysis, providing a set of guiding questions to structure the examination of data, and ensuring a balance of both quantitative and qualitative data. But in my most recent shift toward progress monitoring meetings with teachers and the development of action logs for specific students, I have found another key to this data work that keeps the sense of urgency created by data alive for the teacher and coach: formative assessment tools.

By formative assessment tools, I refer to the formal and informal methods of gathering ongoing assessment data about students in the classroom as action plans are carried out. Some resources, such as the Early Numeracy Interview (Victoria Department of Education, Employment, and Training, 2001) and First Steps in Mathematics (www.stepspd.com/us/index.asp), provide tools and tasks that can be administered to track student growth relative to specific areas of numeracy. Teacher-developed formative assessments specific to the goals established for a student are also valuable as are anecdotal or classroom observation notes as the student works on a task. My work as a coach now includes supporting teachers in this ongoing formative assessment of students. It is an interesting evolution of my work as a coach—shifting my role as coach to encompass diagnostician and data manager as I support teachers in analyzing and organizing their ongoing assessment data to determine next steps for students—but it is also an evolution that makes sense given the larger context of education today.

This discussion of the use of data in coaching at the level of individual student may seem on the surface to focus at a very microlevel—meaning one student at a time. How can this be an efficient use of the coach's time with a teacher when there is an entire class of students to consider? Ultimately, the student-specific conversations that develop from this use of data require that the teacher consider the implications at the macrolevel—meaning classroom instructional practices and structures—in order to implement interventions or action plans for an individual student. Individual student data are objective and neutral; they set the common ground from which the coaching conversation can build. Data can bring the teacher and coach together into a problem-solving dialogue with student learning as the shared goal.

FINAL THOUGHTS ABOUT DATA

Let me close this chapter with one other point regarding the use of data. Monitoring and using data as a coach—both student data and data with regard to teacher learning and growth in practice—is critical from the perspective of demonstrating the impact of coaching. This may be data in the form of qualitative scripts or video clips of a teacher's math lessons gathered at various points along the coaching work or targeting an agreed-upon professional learning focus between teacher and coach. This may be data in the form of student test scores (pre- and postassessments) or student work samples. This may be data in the form of mathematical tasks, problems, or questions posed to students by the teacher (pre- and post-coaching sessions) to illustrate the growth in the level of thinking, rigor, and cognitive demand in the classroom. Some teachers in the midst of a coaching relationship may need this data and explicit opportunities to reflect for themselves on the impact of the coaching sessions in order to sustain their commitment to the work. Moreover, being able to provide evidence of the effectiveness of coaching both in terms of teacher growth and student achievement is becoming more and more necessary to secure continued support and funding for coaching given the local, state, and national climate of accountability.

Questions for Reflecting and Linking to Practice

1. How can the use of data described in this chapter be integrated into the coaching cycle presented in Chapter 3 and the use of curriculum as a coaching tool in Chapter 4?

2. How does the notion of coaching through students described in this chapter compare to the coaching models and coaching cycle described earlier in this book? What are the differences and what are the commonalities across all of these models?

3. In this chapter's case, Peggy unexpectedly did not revert to excuses when presented with her students' data. But how might a coach respond when a teacher does make excuses for poor student performance data?

PART III

Coaching Dilemmas

Confronting Classroom Errors

Mathematics coaches may find themselves in a classroom when an erroneous mathematical idea is put forth (unknowingly) by the teacher. This presents a dilemma for the coach, who shares responsibility with the teacher for the development of accurate and valid mathematics for students in that classroom while simultaneously working to establish and maintain trust and a respectful relationship with the teacher. What are the options or potential moves for the coach as she navigates this situation? What issues emerge as critical to think about? Are there steps that a coach can take to minimize the likelihood that such a situation will occur? These are the questions that will be examined and addressed in this chapter through a pair of coaching encounters that illustrate the diverse approaches that a coach may take in such situations and the variety of factors that impact the coach's decision making.

Case: Keeping the Mathematics in Mind ∞ Holly, Grade 3

In this case, an error emerged as students offered a response that, while correct in a narrow sense, had the potential to create mathematical misconceptions that would need to be undone in later years. I reminded myself of the coach's responsibility to maintain the integrity of the mathematics in the classroom and then I engaged the students themselves, with the teacher, in the process of uncovering the error.

SETTING THE STAGE

Holly's third graders had spent much time over the course of the year studying landmark numbers, such as 10, 25, and 100, that are easy to work with in the base-10 number system and such familiar contexts as money. They had become fluent with the factors of 100 and how to apply knowledge of these factors to other problems, particularly emphasizing the connections to money. On this day, I sat listening to Holly's launch as she posed to the group the following problem:

Holly: Three children need to share $1.00. How much will each child get?

Holly used a think-pair-share technique to engage all students in actively thinking about the problem. As she and I circulated to listen in as pairs shared their thinking on the meeting area rug, I heard multiple pairs sound off with a confident "Impossible." It seemed as if this response of impossible had been used before in the classroom, as if it belonged as a label to a particular set of problems.

When Holly brought the group together again to share their pair thinking, Mark raised his hand and gave that confident response of "Impossible," with affirming nods from many others in the group. Holly nodded as well and smiled; she then asked Mark to explain how he knew this was impossible. Mark explained, quite eloquently, that since $1.00 is like 100, and since three is not a factor of 100, then you can't divide $1.00 with three people. So, he concluded, it is impossible. Holly seemed ready to move on.

DECIDING TO CONFRONT

I began thinking about the mathematics that was ahead for these third graders, namely, the work they would do with division and remainders in fourth grade and beyond. Though $1.00 cannot be divided evenly with three people, it is a problem that has a solution; it is a solution that entails making a decision about how the remainder of one penny is dealt with in the context of the problem. Considering the problem to be impossible not only has the potential of creating misconceptions that will have to be overcome in further study of division, but it also limits the depth of mathematical reasoning and dialogue that could emerge from the problem.

Similar misconceptions and limitations occur when teachers insist that "you can't subtract the bigger number from the smaller number" (you can, but the result will be a negative number), or when they tell students that "multiplication always makes a bigger number" (this is not true if you multiply by zero, one, or a decimal-fraction less than one). The intention is perhaps admirable—teachers want to simplify the mathematics for students, thinking it will be more accessible for students, but the result has implications for future learning. Mathematics isn't always about being simple and we need to let our students grow comfortable grappling with the "messiness" that some mathematical problems present.

So while I understood Holly wanted to focus on applying knowledge of the factors of 100 here with her third graders, I had an eye for the larger mathematical landscape that lay ahead for students (Fosnot et al., 2001). As a math coach, I needed to have the big picture in mind and I had a responsibility to make certain that we all kept an eye on that big picture. It felt like this "impossible" response could not be a response that stood unchallenged in the classroom, as it would narrow children's thinking and require that misunderstandings be reworked in later years. As a coach, you sometimes make a decision to interject in order to preserve the integrity of the mathematics and with an eye for the mathematics that is ahead for students. That was the decision I made.

MAKING THE MOVE

I knew that grounding my challenge of this "impossible" response in student thinking would be one way to approach the issue. Harnessing student thinking can often be the most effective way to engage students and promote learning for both students and the teacher in a nonthreatening way when an error in the math class occurs. All of the pairs I had listened to seemed satisfied with their response of impossible but it seemed to be a response that was a parroting of a response from a previous day's discussion, as if the students felt it was the response that Holly would want to hear. I hadn't heard any pair argue differently about the problem, but I had only had the chance to listen to a handful of pairs. I also had enough confidence in the thinking of third graders to believe they could reason through this work at a different level if some further probing questions were put forth to push their thinking to consider the problem in another way.

Before Holly moved on with the lesson, I decided to interject with a question:

KRW: Ms. Martin, could I ask a question? . . . I'm hearing so many of you agree that this is an impossible problem, but I'm wondering if it really is impossible. Did anyone think about a time when maybe they really did have a dollar to share with three friends? What would you do?

Most of the group was silent but before I could even finish my question, there was one pair on the far side of the rug that was squirming and smiling to each other and both of their hands were waving at me. My trust in the thinking of third graders was right on. Not everyone had seen this as impossible. Now I needed to facilitate this sharing so both Holly and the other students could grapple with the idea. I asked Natalie, one of the two waving an arm in the air, to share what she was thinking.

Natalie: We said you could share it but just not all of it. . . . I mean, you share most of it but someone gets an extra penny. Or you give it to the principal or something.

Others were quiet as they thought about this. Then they too started to agree. I looked at Holly. She was quiet too—thinking, I believe—and then she looked at me.

Holly: So that's the way to think about this?

KRW: Well, we want to think about the problem in a way that makes sense. (I turned back to the class.) So it's not possible to share the dollar evenly and use all of it, but it is possible to share it and then figure out what to do with the extra penny. Because there are times when you have to share money and it doesn't come out evenly. Has anyone ever had that happen to them before?

Holly was able to pick up the discussion at that point as students began connecting to experiences they had had with sharing "leftovers" or remainders. They also began discussing what the options might be for the extra money when you encounter a sharing problem with $1.00 that does not involve a factor of 100. I noted to myself the rich conversations I could have later with Holly about the link to other types of sharing situations, such as sharing brownies, sharing balloons, and more, and how the context might impact the decision about what to do with the extras.

TAKING A CLOSER LOOK

Why in this instance with Holly was I comfortable interjecting? In other situations, I might have felt awkward calling attention to the error and I may have avoided bringing it up for discussion at that very moment in the classroom. But in this case, Holly and I had a very trusting, solid relationship. It was March and we had been working together since September on a regular basis. She was always open to a visit to her classroom and always willing to be candid about her own need to grow mathematically. I knew that she would not be threatened by an interjection I might make in the class; in fact, I knew that she welcomed my participation in her math lessons. We had discussed this in coaching sessions as well; she had given me permission to speak up anytime in class, and this included errors.

Knowing we had discussed such situations explicitly beforehand, I felt very confident interjecting as if we were peers modeling a respectful mathematical discussion in the classroom for the students to hear and be a part of. Not all instances are quite like that, as we'll see later in this chapter.

The mathematical error of this lesson was also successfully navigated due to the manner in which it was approached. That is, rather than confronting the situation from the perspective of telling the teacher in a tone of authority that "impossible" was not an acceptable response, the response was opened for all in the class to think about. This was done through a probing question that elicited another line of thinking about the sharing situation and engaged all students (and the teacher) in reasoning through the mathematical arguments being made. The value of this approach is described below:

> In class, a glaring error may also be addressed by presenting a counter thought and asking the class to consider how those two ideas can both be true. The authority for correctness lies in the mathematical logic and reasoning. Students, teacher, and coach should all engage in the logic and reasoning of mathematics and back away from identifying authorities as absolutes and the source of knowledge. (SVMI, 2007a)

When there is this sense of navigating through the error together with the goal of learning and clarifying understanding, the coach can address errors or problematic situations in the classroom openly and in a manner that is not threatening to the teacher.

In some cases, rather than interject in the moment to call explicit attention to an error, a coach may choose to pull over to the side of the classroom with the teacher to discuss an error. The teacher can then revise his lesson to address the error in the classroom himself, which can be important for those teachers still wrestling to give themselves permission to be learners in the classroom. There are also those instances in which the coach decides that the discussion about an error or problematic situation in the classroom needs to be addressed not in the moment of the lesson but in a postlesson conversation with the teacher. Let's turn to a coaching encounter of that type now.

Case: Deciding When to Address an Error ∞ Maggie, Grade 5

In this case, the error that occurred in the classroom was in the realm of pedagogy, rather than mathematical content. The lack of manipulatives in the classroom prevented fifth graders from modeling three-dimensional space when determining volume. I needed to consider the broader implications for students beyond the single lesson. At the same time, I needed to consider my delicate relationship with this teacher. I could then make a decision as to when and how to address the error.

SETTING THE STAGE

I walked into Maggie's classroom for the final 15 minutes of the class period. It was still early in the year and it was my first year working specifically with the fifth-grade team. I was very much in the midst of establishing relationships and simply being visible to the team members. I was coming into classrooms periodically throughout September to ensure that they had the materials they needed, to address any immediate questions they had as they worked within a lesson, and to gain insights myself into the pulse of each teacher's classroom. Maggie was a veteran teacher on the fifth-grade team, and the district was implementing a new standards-based mathematics program as its core delivery system of curriculum for the first time this year. Maggie had many concerns and trepidations about the new program; while she was appreciative of all support and discussion at weekly team meetings, I was still unsure how the implementation was being translated in her classroom.

I arrived to find that the class was in the midst of an opening session of a three-dimensional geometry and measurement unit. Specifically, they were examining the layered structure of three-dimensional rectangular prisms in order to determine the volume of the prisms. The students had each made a $3 \times 4 \times 3$ inch rectangular prism out of paper (Figure 8.1). Their task was to predict the number of inch cubes that would be needed to fill the box and then to determine the actual number of cubes needed.

Figure 8.1   3×4×3 Rectangular Prism

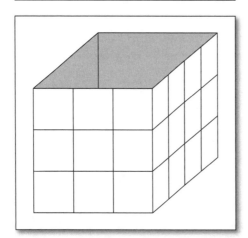

I was pleased to find that Maggie was using the lessons from the unit; in this case, such a hands-on approach to understanding volume was a new way for her to approach what she had previously taught procedurally as the formula "length × width × height." Many of the students were eager to share their predictions. Some had recognized the layered structure of the boxes and so predicted that since the bottom layer would hold 12 cubes and there were three layers, the prism would hold a total of 36 cubes. Others could not yet visualize these layers in the prism; instead, they seemed to look at the outside faces of the box as they turned the box around and around before making a prediction. Their predictions ranged from 12 to more than 60 cubes. I was interested to see what would happen when they filled the paper boxes. The most powerful learning occurs at that moment of cognitive conflict when what one thinks (or has predicted) will happen does not. By predicting and then filling the boxes with cubes, this lesson was designed to allow that to happen.

Then I realized what was missing in all of this. Inch cubes. I looked some more. I walked quietly over to the back counter. Still, I could find no inch cubes visible anywhere in the classroom and certainly not on any of the students' desks. How was Maggie planning to proceed?

After all of the predictions were made, Maggie stood in front of the class with a $3 \times 4 \times 3$ paper prism that she had made to match the students' prisms. She held up one sample of an inch cube and proceeded to demonstrate to the class how that single block might be visualized inside the box. She then asked students to try to count the number of inch cubes that would fill their box. I continued to look for a bucket of inch cubes. I knew that I had delivered these to Maggie earlier in September to be sure that she had all of the materials for the new program. How could students do this without the cubes? Some students repeated their reasoning of the layered structure within the prism. Others continued to count the cubes they visualized in a random manner, with no understanding of the underlying structure of the prism. Maggie then announced the correct number of cubes to the whole class and modeled that solution by moving her single block across the inside of the prism as she spoke. Students recorded this answer and then were assigned several others for homework from a student activity sheet.

DECIDING TO CONFRONT

As Maggie left with her students to bring them to their music period, I remained in her classroom wondering how and even if to address this with her. It was still so early in the year and so early in the relationship that we were building that I wondered if asking her about the lack of manipulatives (inch cubes) in this lesson would only jeopardize my future work with her. Maybe, I thought, this should be a discussion for later in the year, when I have established a stronger relationship with Maggie if I have not seen any growth. At the same time, the new district mathematics program was grounded in the use of manipulatives and other tools for representing mathematical ideas in order for children to build deep, robust conceptual understandings, not merely rote procedures or formulas. The fact that Maggie did not use the inch cubes that day made me wonder if in other lessons the related manipulatives were omitted as well. As I glanced around the classroom again, I did not see any of the buckets of materials that I had distributed to the teachers at the start of the school year—no snap cubes, no color tiles, and no transparent polygons.

So while I was originally tempted not to address this head-on with Maggie that day because I knew it would need to be approached very carefully given the tentative nature of our relationship at that point, I began to realize that the issue was much bigger than simply this one lesson and that it was an issue that would impact student learning beyond that day's math class. I needed to speak with Maggie about the role of manipulatives in math class. Ignoring this would imply a message that the manipulatives were not important and would only reinforce her decision not to use them during the lessons. When student learning is at the forefront, it is not a matter of *if* an error should be addressed or not, but rather a matter of *when* and *how*.

I was glad that I had not raised the issue in the midst of the class session, for that would certainly have jeopardized my relationship with her and it would also not have changed the lesson since there were no materials available. It seemed better to wait until after the lesson to have a conversation one-on-one with Maggie to discuss the role of manipulatives. But still, I began to feel that awkward feeling in my stomach even before she returned to the classroom. How was I going to phrase my words to her about this?

MAKING THE MOVE

I knew I could confront Maggie with a directive about using the manipulatives, but I also knew that what would most likely result would be compliance, especially when I was in the classroom with her for coaching sessions, and a passive compliance with little investment in or understanding of the manipulatives. I needed to approach the issue with Maggie in a way that would prompt her to consider how the inch cubes may have supported her students in their work to determine the volume of the prisms. Did she realize that asking students to determine the actual volume by visualizing without any cubes themselves was, for many students, no different and no less abstract than making a prediction? I needed to keep this grounded in the students; that would convey to Maggie, I hoped, that our shared interest was student learning, and perhaps it would prevent her from viewing our discussion as an attack on her or a lack of respect for her years of experience.

When Maggie returned, I decided to start the conversation with a question about her observations of the student work and thinking, conveying validation of her efforts to work in the new unit.

KRW: It was great to be able to see that part of the lesson today. How have the students been doing with the work in this unit?

Maggie: I know what you want them to do. . . . I know at the meeting we talked about how we want them to be able to see the layers but so many of them just can't right now. They really can't.

KRW: I could hear that in the predictions they made.

Maggie: That's why I was showing them how to imagine the cubes in the box.

KRW: Right. I'm wondering though if they needed to have actually filled the box with the cubes. Then they really could make the layers and see them and start to understand how the box is structured.

Maggie: I thought the cubes would just be too hard for them to manage. I figured I could just show them.

KRW: What are you thinking now?

Maggie: It's a lot of stuff all over the desks, but they aren't seeing the layers. So you think it would help if I have them use the cubes tomorrow?

KRW: I think you should try it and see; then we can talk more about it. Why don't you show me where they are in your classroom so we can check and be sure you have enough of them for tomorrow.

TAKING A CLOSER LOOK

If I walked into Maggie's math class the next day, would it look any different? Maybe. Would Maggie now make use of manipulatives in her math lessons? Maybe sometimes. Did she understand the purpose of these manipulatives and the role they could play in developing concepts for students? Not necessarily to any greater extent than before our conversation. Then what was the impact of my conversation? It put the idea on the table for future discussion. It will be a lesson and a situation that I can return to in future conversations about manipulatives in math class. When I return to her classroom for coaching sessions, she will know that I expect to see students working with manipulatives and she won't be surprised when I push her to think further about these manipulatives in the context of math lessons.

I was pleased. It was a brief coaching encounter, but it was an important one to be had. By waiting until after class, when we could speak together one-on-one, I could prepare my thoughts and navigate the moment in a manner that preserved the relationship I was building with Maggie but without ignoring the mathematical issues that were important to raise in the name of student learning. It was not so much an error in mathematical content here, but rather one of pedagogy and implementation of curriculum. The issues then are deeper and will take more time to truly address, but confronting the error, including an error of this type, is a significant first step.

BEING PROACTIVE: DISCUSSING HOW TO ADDRESS AN ERROR

As mentioned earlier, both in this and previous chapters, it is critical in coaching meetings with teachers to have explicit conversations with each other about the roles that each of you will play during a coach's visit to the classroom. These conversations need to address how errors in the classroom will be handled as well. This establishes a level of trust and comfort for both the coach and the teacher in that, if an error arises in the classroom, there is a shared understanding of how that error will be addressed. If I had addressed the approach to errors more openly and explicitly with Maggie, or even with her grade-level team in team meetings as I began visiting their classrooms informally, some of my discomfort and hesitancy may have been prevented and allowed us to more openly discuss the situation in the moment and redirect the lesson promptly in that class session.

Providing teachers with some ownership in deciding how the errors will be addressed is important, particularly in the early stages of building relationships. Some teachers may state that they would prefer that the coach not raise attention to the error in the moment but instead wait to discuss the error privately following the lesson. As trust is built and teachers grow to see themselves as learners and the importance of ensuring valid, accurate mathematics in the classroom, the conversation can be revisited and teachers will most often gradually become more and more comfortable allowing the coach to make an error public in the midst of the class session so that collaboratively they can build student understanding.

All of this speaks to the moral obligation that coaches have to address errors and discuss candidly with a teacher instruction that may be less than acceptable in terms of fostering mathematical learning. This suggests that the role of the coach is to some extent one of provoking discomfort in the teacher. Certainly, building and maintaining safe, trusting relationships with a teacher is critical in coaching work, but so too is creating disequilibrium if a coach's work is to promote growth for a teacher. These roles are not mutually exclusive. That is, as part of the relationship building with a teacher, a coach may make explicit to the teacher the permission to venture into a sphere of discomfort and indicate that this is intentional and purposeful discomfort. The coach can be transparent about provoking disequilibrium through questions and prompts for reflection. This part of the coach's role needs to be acknowledged as such by both teacher and coach if the hard conversations are going to be had.

BEING PROACTIVE: BUILDING MATHEMATICAL KNOWLEDGE TO AVOID ERRORS

Perhaps the most powerful tool for addressing errors in the classroom is building mathematical and pedagogical content knowledge with teachers prior to their classroom instruction in order to prevent an error from occurring in the classroom in the first place. Elementary teacher preparation programs at the university level and state certification requirements may require a single mathematics methods course, but the majority of university coursework and requirements focus on language arts. Many elementary teachers then bring with them a background in literacy from their teacher training programs and are themselves learning mathematics through the curriculum materials in the district. We certainly want teachers to view themselves as mathematical learners alongside their students, but it is important that prework be done for each lesson to ensure that, while teachers are learners, they are not communicating erroneous mathematics to students.

As mentioned in previous chapters, the prelesson coaching conference, planning session, or team meeting provides an opportunity for coaches to engage teachers in "doing the math" of a lesson or unit for themselves. As adult learners, teachers need professional development opportunities to uncover the underlying mathematical concepts that a lesson or unit is based on, recognize how these mathematical ideas connect to later mathematics work that students will undertake, and become aware of the pitfalls and errors that students (and adults) might make related to the mathematics of the lesson. This can result in potential errors in the classroom being tackled head-on in meetings or math discussions among teachers and coaches prior to the lesson with students. Sometimes coaches tackle the mathematics of a unit with a grade-level team rather than at individual coaching conferences, allowing the one-on-one coaching sessions to focus on issues specific to an individual's classroom or practice but still ensuring that teachers are building content knowledge prior to implementing a lesson. With this support for content knowledge and collaborative understanding of the mathematics in a unit, teachers may also be more open to discussing the mathematics—and any errors that might arise—with the coach in the classroom during a lesson.

Earlier chapters of this book have pointed out the importance of teachers developing deep understanding of mathematical content and pedagogy by doing mathematics themselves, looking at student work samples, examining student thinking recorded in scripts, and reading support resources provided by curriculum materials. But this chapter serves as yet another reminder of the critical need to build teacher content and pedagogical knowledge in order to prevent teacher mathematical errors in the classroom and to build in teachers a stance of learning when such errors do occur. Resource A lists sources that can be used in ongoing study groups or a professional development seminar series with groups of teachers to support this development of mathematical and pedagogical content knowledge. Such study by groups of teachers will, in turn, strengthen the depth of their experience with a coach.

KEYS TO CONFRONTING ERRORS

The coaching encounters presented in this chapter are not intended to offer a prescribed way of addressing errors in the classroom as a coach. Rather, they illustrate the complexity that surrounds these situations and offer some ideas of the range of responses that a coach might consider. The response of the coach may occur in the classroom in the midst of instruction, in a brief exchange with the teacher off to the side as students are working during the lesson, or in a coaching meeting with the teacher following a lesson.

What the coaching encounters of this chapter also illustrate are the many factors that a coach needs to take into consideration when confronted with a situation involving an error in the classroom. The response that a coach makes needs to be a purposeful decision that considers the range of options for addressing errors and the circumstances of the particular situation. The decision may pit the relationship that has been established with the teacher against the students' development of sound mathematical understanding. And often the decision needs to be made in the span of just a minute—or even seconds—in the midst of a classroom lesson. These are decisions that require not only expertise, skill, and professional judgment, but also courage on the part of the coach.

However the coach approaches the error with the teacher, the emphasis is on teacher growth in mathematical understanding and ensuring that authority in the classroom rests not in any one individual but in the mathematics and reasoning being used. The voice of authority is neither the teacher nor the coach then; it is the mathematics. When this is the culture that is established in the classroom collaboratively between teacher, coach, and students, errors—on the part of student, teacher, or even coach—are readily accepted as opportunities for all to learn.

Addressing a Classroom Error: What to Consider

- The integrity of the mathematics content, both short-term and long-term

  Is the integrity of the mathematical content being compromised for students? Are students potentially leaving the lesson with inaccurate mathematical information or misconceptions about mathematical ideas? How might these misconceptions impact their learning in future years?

- The broad impact on mathematics instruction and student learning

  Is the instructional practice preventing students from constructing deep understanding of mathematical concepts? Is it a practice that could potentially cut across strands of mathematics and so impact student development of understanding and mathematical knowledge broadly?

- The relationship that has been built with the teacher

What is the level of trust that has been developed with the teacher? How will raising the error be perceived by the teacher? How has the teacher responded to other opportunities to be a mathematical learner in coaching sessions or team meetings? This should impact only the when and how and not the if of addressing an error; regardless of the relationship or the tension of addressing an error, all students deserve access to accurate mathematical instruction.

- The norms for addressing errors in the classroom that have been discussed

What explicit conversations about roles in the classroom and addressing errors have occurred with the teacher during coaching meetings? Have there been other instances in the classroom in which an error needed to be addressed? How did the teacher respond to the manner in which that situation was handled?

- Student work or student thinking that might be harnessed to discuss the error

What student work or student thinking is evident in the classroom that could be used as a counterexample or to shed light on the error? How might asking students to explain their thinking raise awareness of an error to debate and challenge? How can students be engaged to uncover the error for themselves? What previous student work or experiences might be called upon to address the error in a nonthreatening way?

Questions for Reflecting and Linking to Practice

1. Several instances of errors were presented in this chapter. What are other instances in elementary math classrooms that have the potential to leave students with misconceptions that will then need to be overcome or unlearned in the future?

2. Consider how you have responded to instances of error in the mathematics classroom. What other possible responses to these errors might you now consider?

3. Might there ever be a time when a coach chooses *not* to confront an error with a teacher? Why or why not, and what might be the ramifications of that decision for the teacher and for the students?

9

Transforming the Demonstration Lesson

Many coaches debate the merits of demonstration lessons. Some speak of demonstration lessons as the core of their work; they visit a classroom and teach a model lesson while the teacher observes. Their position is based on the thinking that a demonstration lesson provides teachers with an image of what powerful mathematics instruction looks like in the classroom. They assert that the demonstration lesson builds trust and promotes the teacher-coach relationship. Other coaches say that they refuse to do demonstration lessons in their work. Their position is based on the thinking that demonstration lessons do not truly contribute to the growth of a teacher. They hold that the demonstration lesson involves the teacher only as a passive observer. The demonstration lesson then leaves the teacher dependent on the coach and does not foster growth that will impact the teacher's own practice and students' learning in the classroom on a daily basis.

For several years, I sided with the latter position, refraining from demonstration lessons as much as possible because I was convinced that they would not empower teachers and would not contribute to the teacher's ability to carry on when I was not there. But as I noticed the complexity of situations with teachers, I found myself wondering if in fact there are times when a demonstration lesson is appropriate. I also found myself considering what structures might be put into place or used to render a demonstration lesson effective in a given situation or as part of a sequence of coaching interactions. In this chapter, we focus on the role demonstration lessons may play in coaching and the work of the mathematics coach as a decision maker in this regard.

Case: To Demo or Not to Demo? ∞ Janet, Kindergarten

In this case, when a kindergarten teacher requested a demonstration lesson, I considered a variety of factors that would influence my response to that request. I structured the demonstration lesson in a way that embedded teacher responsibilities both before and during the lesson. This ensured that the demonstration lesson was structured as a professional growth experience for the teacher, similar to how a coteaching model might be harnessed by a coach.

SETTING THE STAGE

It was my second year of work with Janet and the other two kindergarten teachers in her school. I met with this small group of teachers at monthly, afterschool grade-level meetings. At those meetings, I would provide an overview of an upcoming math unit and we would talk about the experiences with the unit lessons in their classrooms. I also made several full-day visits throughout the year that included time in classrooms.

I received this e-mail from Janet one week prior to my January visit to her kindergarten classroom:

"What I'd really like is for you to come and do the 'Eyes' lesson in my class."

She was asking for a demonstration lesson.

My initial thought was, "No." I wanted Janet to feel supported, but I also wanted her to feel as if she was able to implement the unit lessons herself, not that she was dependent on me. Janet might see the lesson I did as a fine lesson but that did not mean it would lead to any change or growth in her own practice. I had encountered this with some other teachers; I would exhaust myself doing single lessons in one room after another, only to find each time I returned to a classroom that the teacher was proceeding with business as usual. I also worried that doing demonstration lessons in her classroom would put Janet in a passive role during my visits. Still fresh in my mind was an instance of a teacher correcting spelling tests in the midst of my demonstration lesson. I was caught off guard and continued the lesson, but I then needed to address explicitly with the teacher the purpose of the demonstration lesson as one of teacher growth. I didn't think that would happen with Janet, but I was hesitant nevertheless.

One of the advantages of e-mail is that there is an inherent time delay in response; I could take a moment to reflect and compose my thoughts before crafting my response to Janet. And that is when so many other thoughts passed through my mind. Should I consider taking on this request and do the lesson? How would Janet benefit from it? Could it support her growth, and if so, how? How did she think this would foster her growth and understanding of mathematics teaching and learning? Or, was it that she wasn't sure how else my visit to her classroom could be used? Was there actually a way to accept her request, continuing to preserve our relationship and build trust, yet craft the demonstration lesson in a way that would render it a powerful professional learning experience for Janet?

I wondered if in fact I should go ahead and teach the lesson in her classroom. Given my history of interactions with Janet over the past 18 months, her request felt different from other demonstration lesson requests I had received of teachers. It didn't seem to me as if she was making this request simply because she wanted a "free period" or was being resistant in her implementation work. I knew from my work with her that she had come a long way in just this past year and a half in terms of broadening her own notions of mathematics; she had come to see math as much more than simply writing numbers or rote counting for her kindergarten students to practice. She was putting forth genuine effort to implement the units in her classroom and was always willing to talk openly with me about her questions and work with the curriculum.

Yet, from the visits I had made to her classroom, it seemed as if her implementation of the program was still very much being carried out through the more traditional lens of mathematics teaching that she had known previously. She poured over each lesson in the teacher's guide and would use the boldface text as her script in the classroom, but the flavor of the discussions in her classroom remained highly teacher directed, with Janet providing the knowledge that she wanted her kindergartners to learn (based on her reading of the lesson). I wondered if perhaps modeling a lesson in her classroom would provide Janet with an opportunity to open her ears, her eyes, and her mind to the ideas that her children could bring to the work and the sense they could make of the mathematics for themselves.

I decided I needed to learn more about why she wanted me to teach the How Many Eyes? lesson in her classroom.* Did she have specific questions about that lesson? What would she like to focus on as I facilitated the lesson in her classroom? I really wanted to be sure that we delineated a clear focus

---

*Note: The "How Many Eyes?" lesson is featured in K. Economopoulos & S. J. Russell. (2004). *Counting ourselves and others: Exploring data.* (Investigations in Number, Data, and Space series). Glenview, IL: Pearson Scott Foresman.

and put forth questions she had that could be kept in mind during the lesson. I thought that by defining these questions and a focus ahead of time, she would be a more active and careful observer during the lesson. This felt much different—much better to me—than simply coming into a classroom and doing an isolated model lesson for a teacher. When I sent Janet an e-mail response to confirm that I would facilitate the How Many Eyes? activity in her classroom, I indicated the work that her students would need to do in the unit leading up to that lesson, and I asked her to meet with me on the morning of my visit so we could talk prior to the lesson to establish a focus for her observation of the lesson. This speaks to the notion of setting purpose and defining roles as critical elements of a coaching cycle preconference discussed in Chapter 3.

To Demo or Not to Demo: Factors to Consider

- What is the relationship I have with this teacher? How might a demonstration lesson further build that relationship?
- What is the past history of my experiences and work with this teacher? How has this teacher responded to the work we have undertaken to date or the meetings that we have had together? Is this a teacher who has shown a willingness to take a risk in her own classroom?
- What could this teacher learn from a demonstration lesson?
- If the teacher has requested the demonstration lesson, has the request been made with a clear reason and focus of study in mind with regard to the impact it may have on her own practice?

When I arrived in the morning, Janet brought me over to a wall in the classroom where a chart of drawings of the children's eyes hung; each child had drawn his or her eyes on an index card and glued the card to the chart in one column.

Janet: I had them draw their eyes on the index cards and they glued them on the chart. But I didn't know what I was supposed to do after that.

KRW: Did the children talk about the chart at all?

Janet: No, we pretty much just made it and I hung it on the wall.

This conversation made me wonder what Janet understood about the mathematical ideas that the experience was intended to develop.

KRW: What do you see as the math in drawing and counting eyes?

Janet: I know it's about two-to-one correspondence, but I just don't see how I am supposed to explain that to kindergartners. I mean, how do I teach them to see that?

Janet's response made me think that she had some sense of the mathematical idea in the counting of eyes (or at least she had read the mathematical emphasis section of the lesson) but she was unsure how that idea develops for children. It seemed as if she was interpreting the lesson from her own lens of teaching in which it was her responsibility to explain or tell the ideas to her students in order for them to learn. Janet's question also had me thinking more deeply about how I approach this work with children. In my mind, it wasn't a matter of how to teach the idea to children; it was about how to build on and extend their intuitive understandings and support them in recognizing, thinking about, and articulating relationships they were noticing. Posing questions that would prompt children to consider the relationships between their counts of eyes and the number of children in the group seemed to be the important piece. Now how could I move Janet to realize that through the demonstration lesson?

I suggested to Janet that while I facilitated the lesson, she focus on the questions that I asked to the group and on the ideas that they brought up in their responses. I provided her with a recording sheet for her observation of the lesson; this guided observation worksheet (see Figure 9.1) posed several questions to focus her observation of the lesson and provided space for recording observations. I also asked Janet to identify children in the group whom she would specifically like to hear responses from to gain insights into how they were making sense of the ideas. I suggested that she write down both the questions that I asked and the ideas that those children articulated during the session on the guided observation worksheet so that we could refer back to these when we talked later. All of this would engage Janet as an active observer, a researcher in fact, during the lesson and provide us with some record of the lesson to look back on and examine when we reflected on the lesson together later that afternoon.

MAKING THE MOVE

I began the session with the children by counting noses. Although the group had done this counting of noses many times before with Janet, I wanted them to be able to use the count of noses as a one-to-one correspondence point of reference later in the activity when we moved onto the two-to-one relationship. The group was smaller than usual due to

Figure 9.1   Guided Observation Worksheet

- What **big idea** of mathematics is being developed in this lesson?

- What **models or materials** are used during the lesson to support the development of mathematical ideas for students?

- What **questions** are posed during the lesson to move the mathematical agenda forward for students?

- Document **evidence of student learning** during this lesson. (Include scripts of student dialogue or student comments, observations, etc.)

Something to think about: At what point in the lesson were students learning the most?

extended vacations of some families, so establishing the number of children and noses for the group was an important piece before moving to count the eyes. Janet seemed a bit surprised that I did not simply want to bring the wall chart of eyes to the meeting area and begin with that. Did she recognize that children's development of the idea of two-to-one correspondence with eyes is dependent upon their knowing how many people are in the group on that particular day? The number of eyes would be different than it was on the day the chart was made due to the different number of children present; asking the children to simply ignore the eyes of absent children on the chart would have moved the experience to a level of abstraction that would have been inappropriate for kindergartners. I made a mental note that this would need to be a piece of our post-lesson conversation.

During the 35-minute mathematics session, the children counted noses, counted eyes, drew eyes again on index cards, created another eye chart (this time, only for those who were present that day), and discussed their work as a group. I noticed that Janet was recording notes on the guided observation worksheet throughout the session. I was pleased to see her taking on this role of observer with commitment, and I found myself wondering what she was writing. Was she commenting on children's behavior in the group, or was she in fact focusing on the ideas the children were bringing to the discussion and the questions that I was using to scaffold the discussion? Her notes alone would provide me with insights into the progress that was occurring in the shift toward children's ideas that had been my goal in my meetings with her team for the past year and a half. Janet's notes would let me know if the lens she brought to the classroom and her students had become sharpened as a result of our meetings together. These notes would serve as a formative assessment of my coaching work and they could help inform my next steps with Janet and her team.

DEBRIEFING

I was thrilled after the lesson when Janet commented on a critical question I had posed to the group. After the children had suggested a variety of counting strategies and had arrived at a count of 13 noses and 26 eyes, I had posed the question, "When we counted noses we only counted 13, but when we counted eyes we counted 26. How can that be?" Janet had recorded the responses of two children:

Jonathan: Because there's two eyes for a person, but there's only one nose. So it's less noses.

Michael: $13 + 13 = 26$. Because it's not just one eye. You have 13 eyes and then 13 more eyes.

As Janet read these notes aloud, she commented excitedly, "I couldn't believe it when I heard them say that. They said it! That was great. Then at the end when they counted the 26 eyes on the chart, Gabe said, 'One card for every kid, but two eyes.' I think he was getting it too."

She noted something important here. Now I just wondered if she recognized how different this was than my explaining two-to-one correspondence relationships to the group. This I would need to examine with her through some additional carefully crafted probing questions, again leading her back to her notes about the questioning I used in the lesson and the student responses. This opportunity for deep discussion grounded in student learning presented itself because I had accepted Janet's request for this demonstration lesson and because I had considered the leverage points that could make this demonstration lesson serve as a vehicle for her growth. I began to question my own theories of coaching. *To demo or not to demo* no longer seemed as clear as *yes* or *no*. It all depends.

TAKING A CLOSER LOOK

What I had done was to transform the work with Janet from a demonstration lesson to a coteaching experience; I brought a coteaching framework to the demonstration lesson and it transformed the experience. Coteaching a lesson with a teacher requires that the teacher prepare for the lesson with the coach. The teacher needs to read the lesson ahead of time and is responsible for preparing all of the materials and setting the necessary foundation of student learning and prior experiences for the lesson. The teacher and coach meet before the lesson or discuss the lesson on the phone or via e-mail to outline the manner in which they will share the lesson implementation; this is the prelesson planning meeting. In the e-mail I sent to Janet to respond to her request, I had explicitly stated her responsibility for implementing the sessions leading up to the How Many Eyes? lesson, and I ensured that we had time together that morning before the lesson to discuss the focus and the roles and responsibilities for implementation clearly.

During a coteaching planning conversation, the coach can pose questions to the teacher about the mathematics focus of the lesson, prior knowledge students bring to the lesson, the range of abilities in the classroom, and how best to support this range in the course of the lesson. These planning conversations and questions are a way of modeling the many dimensions of a lesson and student learning that should be considered when planning intentionally for an effective mathematics lesson. For many teachers, this structure of careful planning must be practiced in order to internalize all of the aspects that need to be taken into consideration when planning a mathematics lesson. The guided coplanning alongside a coach can be a very powerful experience for a teacher. In the planning meeting with Janet, I was also able to gain insights into her understanding of the lesson content and pedagogy.

In the planning conversation with a teacher, I also ask the teacher to identify one question about the teaching of the lesson or about student learning that he or she is bringing to the lesson. For instance, a teacher might indicate uncertainty about how to facilitate the debriefing discussion or the sharing of strategies at the end of a lesson. I might suggest then that the teacher launch the lesson, that we both monitor student work during the lesson, and that I facilitate the discussion at the end of the class to model effective strategy discussion and analysis or to model questioning techniques. We could then discuss this particular piece that the teacher observed me lead at a later meeting time. Or I might suggest to a teacher that we check in with each other just before the discussion segment begins in order to talk briefly about the student thinking that should be highlighted and the questions that might be most powerful to pose to the group; the teacher would then facilitate the discussion but be supported by the coach in the planning for that discussion. In the case of Janet, I steered her focus by giving her the observation recording sheet, but what is critical here is that she had an active, focused role as an observer of the lesson and the debriefing time together could then focus on specific elements of the lesson and student learning, not merely global comments such as "That was good."

Whenever I suggest coteaching to a teacher, I make it a point to validate the collaboration as essential to the success of the lesson. "I may bring a math lens to the lesson," I say. "But you know your students. We need both to make a powerful math lesson." The work of coteaching lets teachers know that I am willing as a coach to push up my sleeves and navigate the realities of teaching young children in the classroom right along with them. In some instances, this is about building trust with a teacher who may otherwise think that I have a hidden agenda for my work or that I am there only to evaluate the teaching. Coteaching builds a sense of shared ownership for a lesson and collegiality as we work alongside one another to foster and reflect upon student learning.

I should add here that it's not always as formal as a full cotaught lesson. Sometimes it's asking a teacher to shadow you and listen in as you are working with a small guided math group. Sometimes it's asking the teacher to listen in as you conference with a student about his or her work. In both cases, once the work with the student or small group is complete, the coach turns to the teacher and articulates the rationale and thinking that informed each instructional decision with that child or group during the time. It is this transparency of thinking, modeling purposefulness of actions that is critical.

KEYS TO TRANSFORMING THE DEMO LESSON

The question of demonstration lessons seems to be not so much a matter of whether to do a demonstration lesson or not, but rather a matter of how the coach orchestrates the experience to promote the growth of the teacher. It is that responsibility for the growth of the teacher that needs to be at the forefront of the coach's mind when crafting the demonstration lesson. That is the shift that I find is perhaps the most difficult for many who move out of the classroom to a new role in coaching; in the role of coach, the responsibility is to promote student learning *through* the growth of the teacher. I have mentioned this in other chapters as well, but it merits reiterating.

The planning of a demonstration lesson in the mind of the coach must shift from a focus on the student only to a focus on how best to make one's planning and implementing of a lesson transparent to a teacher and how best to use the lesson as a vehicle for moving teacher practice and reflection to a new level. Many of the elements of a demonstration lesson that promote teacher growth parallel closely what might be seen when coteaching a lesson with a teacher.

- Coach and teacher plan the lesson together beforehand, discussing the mathematics, the student profiles, and the instructional outline.
- Prior to the lesson, the teacher identifies professional focus questions or a dimension of practice that he or she is particularly interested in studying during the lesson.
- The teacher takes responsibility for implementing related classroom sessions both prior to and following the demonstration lesson to ensure that students are experiencing the development of ideas over time, not merely an isolated lesson.
- The teacher's role during the lesson is one of researcher; focus questions on a guided observation worksheet steer the teacher's observations, and the notes the teacher records become the springboard for a focused and specific postlesson conversation in the debriefing meeting.

Clearly, this is harder for the coach and demands a different skill set than simply planning and implementing a demonstration lesson for students. But with the teacher more actively engaged in the prelesson discussions and the recording of classroom observations, and with the teacher defining a purpose for observing the coach in the lesson, there is shared ownership of the lesson. It suggests studying other lessons together and coteaching as valuable and comfortable next steps with the coach. This then repositions the demonstration lesson not as an isolated or one-time experience with a teacher but rather as a piece of the broader relationship that a coach and teacher are building and the ongoing work that they undertake together.

Questions for Reflecting and Linking to Practice

1. Consider how you might make decisions about whether or not to accept a request for a demonstration lesson. Are there factors other than those listed in the case that might be important to consider? What new insights regarding "factors to consider" have you gained from this case?

2. How might you respond or react if a teacher begins to check e-mail, correct tests, or otherwise disengages completely in the midst of a demonstration lesson?

3. Several tools, such as the guided observation worksheet, were noted in the case as vehicles to maintain the ownership, investment, and active participation of the classroom teacher. What other vehicles or tools might be used to focus teachers as active participants in the effective demonstration or coteaching lesson?

10

The Coach as a Learner

Throughout the chapters of this book, we have seen the coach take on many different roles and use many different tools to support teacher growth. Often, I have felt that teachers see my role as expert. On the one hand, I have worked hard to develop a solid knowledge base in mathematics and children's mathematical thinking; this knowledge base gives me credibility in my work. But, on the other hand, there are still many questions that I have about how children's ideas develop and how best to support that learning. I learn more from every visit I make to a classroom and every time I discuss children's work with a teacher. I find myself raising new questions to ponder each time I listen to students working hard to make sense of mathematics. In fact, there are times when it feels as if the more I learn in this work, the more I realize that there is still so much to learn. In other words, I am still a learner, and the very act of coaching itself serves as an opportunity to learn.

Does this role of learner render me any less credible in the eyes of the teachers with whom I work? How do I balance the notion of *coach as expert* with the reality of *coach as learner*? I have heard other coaches raise these same questions and concerns, so it seems that this role of coach as learner is one that is worthy of reflection and discussion.

Case: Doing the Math ∞ Lisa, Grade 5

In my encounter with a fifth-grade teacher, I found myself puzzling over a piece of mathematics she presented to me as a trick she had shown her students. I needed to first give myself time and permission to tackle and unpack the mathematics. Then I needed to consider how to share my new insights with the teacher.

Before moving into this case, I invite you to first do the math for yourself. This is an opportunity to sharpen the lens you bring to the mathematics in the case, just as a coach would ask a teacher to do the math related to an upcoming lesson in the classroom.

The Mathematics

Consider the two fractions below:

9/5   7/4

Which fraction is larger? How do you know? How would you represent your thinking using pictures or a diagram? How would you articulate your reasoning using numbers and words? What other strategies could be used to determine and prove the larger fraction?

Now consider this approach to the fraction comparison:

"If you have 9/5 and 7/4 and you multiply 9 × 4, that's 36 and then you multiply 5 × 7, that's 35. Since 36 is more than 35, you know that 9/5 is more than 7/4."

$$36 \qquad\qquad 35$$
$$\frac{9}{5} \bowtie \frac{7}{4}$$

Why does this work? What thoughts do you have about this approach to the fraction comparison?

SETTING THE STAGE

When I arrived in her classroom, Lisa seemed very frustrated with her students' work in the fifth-grade fractions unit and turned immediately to show me a student sheet of fraction comparisons that she would be using with her students later that day. She asked, with desperation in her voice, "Is it all right if I show them the crisscross trick to figure out which is bigger?"

I was not sure exactly what she meant, so I asked her to explain to me what the trick was.

She explained, "It's like this: If you have 9/5 and 7/4 and you multiply 9 × 4, that's 36 (she wrote 36 above the 9), and then you multiply 5 × 7, that's 35 (she wrote a 35 above the 7). Since 36 is more than 35, you know that 9/5 is more than 7/4."

$$36 \qquad\qquad 35$$
$$\frac{9}{5} \bowtie \frac{7}{4}$$

Lisa continued, "That's the way that I was taught to do it."

I looked at what she had written. I knew this was not what was appropriate for fifth graders to be learning about comparing fractions, but I found it interesting that it worked. I was curious as to what mathematics was underlying this trick. I had a hunch that it had something to do with finding a common denominator, but I was not exactly sure how that explained it. I needed, though, to respond to Lisa in the moment. While I didn't have a ready mathematical explanation for her, I knew it was important to let her know I'd think more about this, just as I had coached teachers to do when they encountered students' strategies that they were not familiar with in the classroom.

KRW: I haven't seen fraction comparisons approached in that way before. I'll have to look at it more closely.

Lisa: It works every time. I know I saw it in textbooks when I was in school. So do you think it's OK for me to show my kids? . . . And why *does* it work anyway?

MAKING THE MOVE

That last question seemed to come out of Lisa's mouth before she could stop it. We both started to laugh about the irony of what she was asking. Here she was asking if she could teach her children a mathematics trick when she herself had no understanding of the mathematics behind the trick. Lisa and I had been working together for the past several months in our coaching sessions to not only look at student work but also deepen her own mathematical content knowledge, so I knew that she had seen the power of having a conceptual foundation, not simply rote procedures.

KRW: Lisa, listen to what you just said. The fact that you're not sure why that cross-multiplying trick works tells me it isn't something that you'd want to just show your students. That is, if your goal is for them to really understand how fractions compare.

Lisa: You're right . . . except, I have to admit, I already did. And of course they grabbed on to it right away! I knew I shouldn't have. Now I'll tell them they have to compare the fractions on this page in another way.

I wanted her to think about the more meaningful strategies that her students could use, grounded in their work in the unit so far.

KRW: How else do you think they could approach the fraction comparisons?

Lisa: They could draw a picture, I guess. But that's not really efficient. That's why I showed them the trick in the first place.

KRW: But for someone who still needs that picture to really get a sense of the fraction, just showing them a trick isn't really going to help it be clearer in their heads.

Lisa: I know . . . you're right. But what about these? (She was referring again to the student sheet items.)

We then considered the comparison of 9/5 and 7/4 that was on the page. I asked Lisa how she thought her students might approach that comparison. At first, she responded with a blank look. I wondered then if Lisa relied so much on the cross-multiplying trick she had been taught that it was difficult for her to fathom her students having any other strategies to draw on in the work.

After a moment of silence, Lisa offered an idea.

Lisa: Well, maybe they'd see that 5/5 is a whole so then there's 4/5 left. And 4/4 is a whole, so there's 3/4 left. But then they have to compare 4/5 to 3/4.

KRW: And how do you think they would do that?

Lisa: They'll use decimals, 0.8 and 0.75.

I was glad to hear that at least she recognized the unit was encouraging students to develop connections among fractions, decimals, and percentages and that some students may find it helpful to move from one to the other.

KRW: Do you think anyone might visualize a number line model and use a fraction benchmark? Could they think about how far 4/5 and 3/4 each are from a whole? That 4/5 is just 1/5 from a whole but 3/4 is 1/4 from a whole, so 4/5 is closer to a whole and must be larger than 3/4?

This seemed to overwhelm Lisa. She replied, "Gee, I don't know. I don't think my kids would ever think about it like that!"

Her students were returning from the library, so our time to talk came to a sudden close. I wanted to talk more to Lisa about her students' strategies and about reasoning with fractions. I wondered if she needed to become more comfortable with using a number line model and benchmark fractions in comparisons in order to see the significance of that strategy. Like so many of us, her experiences with fractions in school had been much different. Thinking that students can reason about fractions in this way can be hard to imagine when it is not the way that we ourselves came to think about fractions. We planned to meet the next morning during her prep time. I told her that I was interested in thinking more about the trick and that I'd share with her my thoughts to see if we could uncover why it works too.

DOING THE MATH

I was excited to spend some time digging into this cross-multiplying technique and uncovering the mathematics of it. That evening I sat down to look closely at the trick. I began by applying the cross-multiplying technique to several simpler fraction comparisons to see if I could uncover what was happening mathematically and if it was related to my hunch about common denominators. I began with comparing 1/3 and 1/4. Yes, the cross-multiplying technique worked for these fractions as well.

$$4 \qquad\qquad 3$$
$$\frac{1}{3} \quad\diagdown\kern-0.8em\diagup\quad \frac{1}{4}$$

(1 × 4 = 4 and 1 × 3 = 3; 4 is more than 3 and 1/3 is more than 1/4)

I noticed that 1/3 is equivalent to 4/12 and 1/4 is equivalent to 3/12. Comparing the numerators of those fractions was the same as comparing 4 to 3. My common denominator hunch seemed to be on the right track.

I tried another, this time comparing 3/4 to 1/2.

$$6 \qquad\qquad 4$$
$$\frac{3}{4} \quad\diagdown\kern-0.8em\diagup\quad \frac{1}{2}$$

Again I could see that 6 is more than 4 and 3/4 is greater than 1/2. Now the connection to a common denominator was becoming clearer to me: 3/4 is equivalent to 6/8; 1/2 is equivalent to 4/8. I could see now that the cross-multiplying technique was grounded in expressing the fractions with a common denominator (though not necessarily the least common denominator), but that the notation used (recording just the numerator of the equivalent fraction above the fractions being compared) masked this. The common denominator is not recorded in the notation used.

To create the common denominator, the denominators of the fractions being compared are multiplied (thereby not necessarily resulting in the least common denominator). The resulting product is a multiple of both original denominators and so can be used as a common denominator when renaming the fractions. Cross-multiplying essentially renames each original fraction with the common denominator just found because it multiplies the numerator by the same number that the denominator was multiplied by to arrive at the common denominator. This is also the same as multiplying by 1 (for instance, multiplying $3/4 \times 2/2$) and is creating a fraction equivalent to the original fraction but expressed with a common denominator.

I returned to the original comparison of 9/5 and 7/4 that Lisa and I had looked at to "see" this:

$$\frac{9 \times 4 = 36}{5 \times 4 = 20} \qquad \frac{7 \times 5 = 35}{4 \times 5 = 20}$$

36/20 is greater than 35/20; therefore, 9/5 is greater than 7/4.

Here, it is not simply that the 9 has been multiplied by 4—as appears in the cross-multiplying notation—but the 5 has also been multiplied by 4 to create the equivalent fraction. Therefore, 9/5 is being multiplied by 4/4 or 1. The same is the case in terms of both the 7 and the 4 being multiplied by 5, such that 7/4 is being multiplied by 5/5 or 1.

All of this is not apparent in the shortcut notation of simply writing the product of cross-multiplying above the original fraction. I liken this to the mathematical ideas (place value) that are embedded but hidden in the "carry the one" notation in operations with whole numbers. This suddenly seemed very obvious to me. I wonder if the fact that I had first seen the trick demonstrated with fractions larger than 1 had made it more difficult for me to reason through the mathematics involved. Analyzing cross-multiplying with the simpler, more common fractions seemed to make the mathematics involved much more obvious to me and I was then able to apply it to the other fractions.

TAKING A CLOSER LOOK

As a teenager, I remember being "good" in math because I could memorize the tricks, and this fit the traditional schooling that I was raised with. But I also knew that I didn't truly understand why the formulas I memorized worked or how they would ever apply to the real world. So when my freshman calculus professor in college asked me to consider a major in mathematics, I laughed and responded truthfully, "I did well in your course because I could memorize everything you did. I don't understand a bit of it." It wasn't until I became an elementary teacher and began listening to how children thought about mathematical ideas and thinking about how these ideas develop in children that I realized that mathematics was meant to be a sense-making experience. It wasn't until I was a graduate student in a mathematics leadership program and took higher-level mathematics courses taught in the manner that they hoped all of us taught our students that I realized that understanding complex, abstract concepts in mathematics was not reserved for an elite few but was accessible to all when the appropriate environment and instruction was provided. I memorized the formula for the derivative in my high school calculus class. I memorized it again in my college calculus class. As a graduate student, we measured the speed of cars as they traveled various distances down Broadway on the Upper West Side of New York City, and from these calculations, I could, for the first time, make sense of a derivative as more than just an arbitrary formula to be memorized.

In that way, I learned that there can be great satisfaction in examining a mathematical procedure and puzzling over it until figuring out why it worked. That is why I felt so invigorated and excited to look at the mathematics that night after hearing Lisa describe the fractions trick. I knew that there was a reason—a reason grounded in the mathematics—for why it worked, and I believed that if I worked through it long enough, I could uncover that reason. I literally could not wait to get home and get to work on my own math "homework" that night.

PERMISSION TO BE A LEARNER

I had felt this same excitement in the classroom as a teacher when students raised a new approach to a problem and I wanted to understand why their approach worked (and if in fact it was grounded in sound mathematics). But I have to admit that I found it much easier to model this stance of a learner for students as a classroom teacher than to do so for teachers as a coach. That is, there were many times in my first years as a coach when I felt extremely uncomfortable acknowledging to a teacher that the question raised was one for which I did not have an answer. Teachers would introduce me to their classes as the "math lady" or the "math expert." I suppose in my mind to admit that I did not know the answer to a question that was raised was a sign of incompetence in my work. If I was the coach, the expert, then I should have all the answers, right?

No. The truth is that mathematics is not a static discipline with a finite body of knowledge for an expert to master. Rather, it is a discipline that is about learning, making sense of the world, and problem solving. Math is not about being an expert; it is about being a learner.

I gradually came to give myself permission to be a learner with teachers even in the role of their coach. So in the case of Lisa, I needed to admit openly that I did not know why her trick worked at that moment of our conversation but that I was excited to look into it further and would. In fact, I was modeling openly for Lisa the approach to learning mathematics that we hope teachers will model for students. Still, this takes honesty and humility on the part of the coach and a breaking down of misperceptions that some teachers may have of coaches.

KEEPING THE TEACHER IN MIND

When you are a coach and a learner, the learning is not only for your own growth but must also be considered in terms of its implications for the growth of the teachers with whom you work and ultimately their students. Certainly, my mathematical work to understand the mathematics behind the cross-multiplying procedure was personally satisfying to undertake. But the key as a coach is being able to return from such a "detour" to focus again on how to foster teacher growth, even at times while still being a learner. I struggled with this in the case of Lisa.

I couldn't wait to share with Lisa all of the mathematical work I had done independently that night to figure out why the trick worked. But then I began to wonder how I should share all of that with her. I wondered if I should have waited and tackled the mathematics of the cross-multiplying procedure with her at our meeting the next day. There was a part of me that preferred looking closely at the trick by myself first; I have always found this to be my learning style, to think carefully and deeply before making my ideas public. Once I had taken some time to work on the problem, I was excited to talk to Lisa about my work, but if I just told her why the trick worked, wouldn't that short-circuit her understanding and result in a missed opportunity to develop a disposition of inquiry? How could I scaffold the work so she could uncover the *why* of the trick without telling her too much? Or would it actually be more productive (and a better use of our limited time) if I just explained what I had learned about the cross-multiplying procedure so we could spend a greater portion of our meeting focusing on her students' work and the meaningful strategies that are appropriate for students to develop? I was thrilled by what I had learned through my own mathematical investigation, but I felt very torn as to how to proceed with Lisa's learning in mind.

What becomes critical in making the decision as to how to proceed is to consider the most powerful learning opportunity for the teacher at that moment. Is it a teacher who is not intimidated by the mathematics and so will be willing to do the math alongside you? Or is it a teacher who would be more willing to open his or her mind to new understandings of mathematics when it comes through a focus on student work and student thinking in the classroom? Is that a less threatening vehicle for studying mathematics and deepening understanding? Time as a coach is often limited in terms of opportunities to engage in conversations with teachers so it is all the more important that decisions be made carefully as to what approach will best match the readiness and needs of the teacher.

In all of this, the modeling of being a learner is important in terms of the big picture as a coach. This entails being open and honest in letting teachers know what you know and what perhaps you are not clear about. And in being open about what it is that you may not know, it is then important to be explicit and public about how you are going to go about finding out more. This may be solving problems and examining the math like a mathematician, much as I did in the case of Lisa. Inviting the teacher to tackle this alongside you or to listen in as you think through the mathematics for yourself may be an easier way for them to be learners and reveal mathematics that they too are working to understand.

Sometimes a coach will need to tackle a piece of learning that falls in the realm of children's development of ideas. For instance, a second-grade teacher came to me asking how to move her students with language disabilities to find ways to effectively communicate their problem-solving strategies. I was as perplexed by this as she was and knew that only through action research that we undertook together in her classroom would the practices that were best for these particular children emerge for us. Inviting a teacher to join you in figuring out the answers to a classroom question he or she has raised can also be an entry point into working with that teacher; it can feel much less intimidating—and ultimately very satisfying—to a teacher to enter into this kind of inquiry with a coach.

KEYS TO BEING COACH *AND* LEARNER

As a leader of change in a school, coaches should consider themselves "lead learners" for the school community as well. The key to being such a lead learner as a coach is modeling the learning stance for teachers and then inviting teachers to be partners alongside you in the mathematical investigation, in the action research, or simply in the conversations about what you know and what you don't know. It is important to not let this learning stance be mistaken for incompetence or a lack of preparation for the coach position. But when it is a learning stance taken in the context of ongoing support to teachers and in a culture of learning, risk taking, and reflecting that is established in a school, it can serve to foster that culture further.

Keys to Being Coach *and* Learner

- Give yourself **permission** to be both coach and learner.
- Model a learning stance; be **open and transparent** with a teacher about what you do know, what you are not sure about, and how you will learn more:

  "I haven't seen that strategy before. Let me take a closer look at it."
  "That's an interesting question. I want to think some more about that."

- **Consider vehicles that allow the teacher to join you in the learning,** perhaps collaboratively investigating the mathematics or undertaking action research with you in the classroom to examine a question that has emerged.

(Continued)

(Continued)

- **Model** (through think-alouds, e-mails, etc.) how you are undertaking the work to study the strategy or issue further, the questions that it raises for you, and the hypotheses you are making along the way.
- As you learn, **keep in mind the implications for the teacher's growth and student learning** in the classroom; make decisions for coaching based on teacher readiness and needs.

Questions for Reflecting and Linking to Practice

1. Look back at your own mathematics work with the fractions 9/5 and 7/4. What new insights or additional thoughts do you have about the comparison of these and other fractions after reading the case? (*Author's Note*: I have since talked to others about the cross-multiplying procedure. It was pointed out to me that the mathematics of ratio and proportion is related to all of this; in a proportion, the product of the means equals the product of the extremes. This connection was not obvious to me at the time of my work with Lisa, and this is mathematics that I am continuing to think about.)

2. At the end of this case, the dilemma is presented as to how to approach next steps with the fraction comparisons with Lisa. How would you proceed? Why?

3. What other challenges and emotions have you encountered, or might you anticipate, as you navigate the perception of coach as expert versus the reality of coach as learner?

PART IV

Growing the Coach

11

Professional Development for the Coach

The very premise of this book is that elementary mathematics coaches can provide powerful, job-embedded professional development to teachers. But what about professional development for the coach? What sets of skills, knowledge, and strategies must an elementary mathematics coach develop and refine in an ongoing manner to perform the work effectively? What vehicles of professional development afford the coach opportunities for developing such skills and knowledge? How does a coach grow in his or her practice? Another way of asking this may be: Who's coaching the coach?

This chapter describes a variety of ways that other coaches and I have navigated the reality of developing our coaching practice in districts for which this role is new both to the coach as well as the classroom teachers. We'll examine professional development resources that can support the coach in developing coaching skills and strategies in a safe environment. Some are tools and resources for those who are coaching independently in small districts or schools. Some lend themselves more to the collaboration that can emerge from a cohort of mathematics coaches in a large district. All of these tools suggest that, although communication and learning styles may differ from one person to the next, there are components of coaching that all people can study, practice, and refine.

IDENTIFYING WHAT COACHES NEED TO KNOW

The first step in developing a responsive professional development plan for mathematics coaches is identifying the essential skills, knowledge, and strategies that are needed for the complex role of coaching. For several years, I was the author and facilitator of an online coaching seminar. Elementary mathematics coaches, staff developers, team leaders, and even administrators from across the country (and sometimes outside the country) participated in the eight-week seminar. They read coaching cases and dialogued with each other in facilitated conversations about the moments of coaching embedded in the cases. Through an analysis of participant interviews, archives of coded online postings from the participants, and seminar evaluations, I worked with collaborating researchers to articulate some of the skills, strategies, and supports coaches need to be successful. These are described in Figure 11.1.

Another knowledge base that can be helpful for coaches to have in their toolbox is an understanding of the Concerns-Based Adoption Model (CBAM) (Hord, Rutherford, Huling-Austin, & Hall, 1987). CBAM was first developed at the University of Texas and has been used extensively in staff development, teacher change, and mentorship models. Knowledge of this model can support the coach's understanding of the adult learner and the levels of concern that teachers typically move through in the process of change. For instance, as teachers first move into new work or the beginning stages of a change process, they are often at a level of concern grounded in building awareness of the change and gaining information about what it is. Teachers then move through phases focused on the implications for themselves personally, in terms of skills to be learned. In the later stages, teachers begin to raise questions about how the change impacts students and how collaboration may enhance the work still further. Understanding a teacher's level of concern or stage of development allows the coach to select an approach that is a good fit for a teacher at that given time.

MOVING FROM RESEARCH TO PRACTICE

I know of coaches who formed study groups in their districts as a vehicle to develop their coaching practices. They grounded their study group meetings in readings and text-based discussions of research related to each of the knowledge areas noted in Figure 11.1. As valuable as this study was, however, the question of how to move the knowledge base to practice eventually emerged for members of these study groups.

One group of coaches decided that to move beyond the professional readings about coaching toward putting these ideas into practice, they needed opportunities to rehearse or "have a go" with coaching moves in a setting that supported their approximations and their first attempts.

Figure 11.1   Coaching Knowledge and Skills

INTERPERSONAL SKILLS

Communicating and establishing trusting relationships with teachers who are trying to change their practice requires being sensitive to their dilemmas, fears, and celebrations. Coaches must be able to observe accurately and provide teachers with appropriate feedback about their practices in a respectful and collaborative manner. Coaches also may serve as liaisons between teachers and administrators, requiring that they advocate for teachers while also working with administrators to move forward with specific goals and to create a learning community in the school as a whole.

CONTENT KNOWLEDGE

Coaches must have a deep understanding of subject matter, including how knowledge of a discipline is developed through curricula and learning materials. Experience with coaches at the elementary level indicates that a certain level of content-area expertise is necessary to be a subject-area coach. However, expertise is necessary to be a subject-area coach. However, expertise also may create tension when coaches are labeled experts. Most important is for a coach to establish a collaborative, reflective relationship with a teacher, not to tell the teacher what to do, but serve instead as a knowledge resource and a mediator to help the teacher reflect.

PEDAGOGICAL KNOWLEDGE

To lead, coaches need to understand how children learn, including a deep knowledge of the tasks, questioning strategies, and classroom structures that can help students develop ideas.

KNOWLEDGE OF THE CURRICULUM

Familiarity with the structures and experiences offered by a particular curriculum is essential, including understanding the fundamental ideas behind the curriculum and how those ideas connect across grade levels.

AWARENESS OF COACHING RESOURCES

Coaches need specific knowledge of professional development materials, literature, and resources that can be used to support a teacher's development of subject or pedagogical knowledge or help teachers better understand how to teach for understanding.

KNOWLEDGE OF THE PRACTICE OF COACHING

Coaches must know coaching strategies and structures, such as how to use pre- and postconferences or on-the-spot coaching; the role of questioning and effective strategies; how to use artifacts of teaching practice, e.g., curriculum materials, student work, scripts of classroom dialogue; and the pros and cons of demonstration lessons. Coaches also must understand the multiple roles of a coach in the classroom. For instance, a coach may plan a lesson with a teacher, coteach a lesson alongside a teacher, observe particular students, or create a transcript of a class discussion to examine with the teacher in a postlesson meeting.

Source: From Stephanie Feger, Kristine Woleck, and Paul Hickman. (2004). How to develop a coaching eye. *Journal of Staff Development,* 25(2): 14–18. Reprinted with permission of the National Staff Development Council, www.nsdc.org. All rights reserved.

They began to brainstorm a variety of ways that they could practice coaching in a setting that felt nonthreatening not only to a teacher but also to the coach. They also wanted to find settings that might allow them to receive feedback on their coaching moves and decisions so that they could refine this work before moving into more challenging coaching situations.

To find supportive environments for coaching, it is sometimes necessary to give yourself permission to consider which teachers in a building might be ideal for rehearsing coaching moves. I say *permission* because at first many coaches have an image—an overwhelming image—that they should undertake one-on-one coaching meetings with every teacher in their building immediately. As noted in Chapter 2, "Starting the School Year," narrowing the focus to a small group of teachers, perhaps even just a single teacher for the sake of getting started, can render coaching most focused and effective. It can also allow a coach to develop the skills of coaching with reciprocity from the teacher.

Being explicit with these classroom teachers about the fact that you are trying out coaching and working to develop your skills as a coach can also be valuable. Even for some of the most willing classroom teachers, the reflective questions that a coach poses during a coaching meeting may be unfamiliar. The teacher may believe that the coach already has answers in mind; the teacher will try to read for cues from the coach rather than realize the purposeful nature of the questioning as a tool to push for deeper reflection. With this in mind, a coach might delineate this focus explicitly to a teacher:

> I'm trying out some of the ideas from my coaching study group. I'll be asking you questions that might seem unfamiliar and maybe even uncomfortable at first, but they are a way for us to push our thinking and reflection about student learning and practice to a new level together.

COACHING SIMULATIONS

Some of this work to rehearse, or practice, coaching in a safe environment might also come in the form of coaches coaching each other; that is, members of a coaching study group practicing coaching conferences and coaching moves with each other. Two members of a group of math coaches I worked with found this particularly valuable. One implemented a lesson in a classroom while the other observed and the two met after the lesson for a debriefing meeting between "coach" and "teacher." This provided an opportunity to have authentic instruction and student work to ground the conversation, but coaching questions could be posed and coaching moves made with a colleague who was herself reflective and so could respond in ways that fed the conversation.

The two coaches then stepped out of their roles to debrief the coaching conference from the perspective of the effectiveness and impact of the decisions, questions, and moves that were made; each could be transparent with the other about the experience. Together, they considered alternate coaching decisions, questions, or moves that might have been made along the way, and they also brainstormed alternate responses that another teacher, particularly one who was more resistant or who had had less experience reflecting on practice, might have put forth. Both said this collaborative coaching simulation allowed them to rehearse coaching moves, offer each other powerful constructive feedback, and gain confidence in their repertoire of coaching skills.

JOURNALING AS A TOOL FOR LEARNING

In my first coaching experience, I worked in a small district in which I was the only K–8 mathematics coach; what's more, it was the first time this district had such a position. While I found the opportunity to craft the position stimulating and invigorating, it was also a bit daunting. I quickly realized that I needed a tool that would allow me to process all that I was undertaking and support my reflection on my work. Writing became my own professional development tool.

I kept a journal and each night I would record a piece of my day. Some nights this writing would be my reflections about a transcript of dialogue I had recorded in a classroom that day. Some nights I would recall an interaction with a teacher that day and note my feelings of frustration or satisfaction at the moves I had made. Over time I began to revisit my journal notes and I would develop past entries further based on more recent interactions I had with that teacher or based on new perspectives I had developed. Some of these entries I handwrote in a journal as I sat in bed at night. Some I typed on my laptop. It was not so much the form the product took that was critical but the thinking and reflection that surrounded the writing.

When you are in the midst of a coaching interaction, often the situation unfolds very quickly and it becomes difficult in the moment to realize the significance of each decision or move. Writing pushes the author—the coach—to become more aware of each decision that is made and consider the implications, alternatives, broader context, and potential next steps for the coaching work. In this way, journal writing can serve as a vehicle for revisiting and processing a coaching experience, looking objectively at the interaction, and reflecting on the moves and decisions that were made; the writing is not an evaluative piece of writing but rather is undertaken in the spirit of self-reflection and growth.

BELONGING TO A COACHING COMMUNITY

During my first years of coaching, I also began to seek out professional development experiences with coaches in other districts. I had the support of the elementary and middle school mathematics curriculum coordinator in my district. But I needed to reflect on my work in collaboration with colleagues who were engaged in parallel work, confronting the same challenges and celebrating the same successes as I was, however small. I needed to be able to share the range of emotions that accompanies coaching—frustration, doubts, excitement, and passion for the work—and to have these emotions validated by others experiencing them. I needed to belong to a wider coaching community.

I began to share writing from my journal in the form of two- to three-page coaching cases at a study group of coaches from nearby districts. This provided me with an authentic audience for my coach's journal. As members of the study group responded to the writing and offered their perspectives and thoughts, I was able to revisit the coaching interactions and moves again with fresh eyes. Others in the group also shared their own coach writing. We shared these coaching cases from our work not as exemplars of coaching but rather as artifacts of our work that would allow us to ground discussions in a shared point of reference in order to discuss common themes of our work, unpack the dilemmas that we encountered, and reflect on the range of moves and decisions that may be made before being confronted with a similar situation in the moment of a coaching challenge.

This sharing of coaching cases, with a set of focus questions composed for each case by the coach-author, served as extremely powerful professional development. It becomes easy as a coach to focus so intently on the professional development for others that you lose sight of the need to give time for your own professional development. Study groups, case writing, and case reading and analysis with other coaches are all forms of job-embedded professional development for coaches. These experiences allow coaches to make the practice of coaching transparent and this transparency allows coaching to be studied collaboratively.

In districts that have large cadres of coaches, a weekly or biweekly coaches' meeting is often built into the coach's schedule. At these facilitated coaches' meetings, coaches may engage in some mathematics (to expand their own content knowledge), look at curriculum resources, and examine student learning from the classroom. However, to study the practice of coaching itself at these meetings, cases from an external source or publication or from the writing of a member of the coach group can be the most powerful learning artifact for a team to read, discuss, and connect to their own situation.

In the case of a small district or a district with just one or two math coaches, partnerships with other districts taking on this work is one option for collegial dialogue. Partnering with a coach in the district who is responsible for a different curriculum area, such as language arts or science, is another possibility. While curriculum content may not be the focus of those conversations, issues of coaching that transcend curriculum areas can be discussed, with new perspectives and connections often uncovered in these cross-curricular conversations. Online seminars and online communities targeting the professional needs of mathematics coaches specifically and instructional coaches broadly have also emerged over the past 5 to 10 years, and research studies of these online experiences point to the power of peer-to-peer (in this case, coach-to-coach) interactions for professional growth (Feger & Woleck, 2007).

Professional development for math coaches is still in its early stages. Fortunately, the body of literature is growing to provide coaches with print resources to foster their own growth and professional development. Institutes and seminars, both face-to-face and in virtual or online environments, have also been developed. Resource B provides an overview and some examples of the various types of professional development resources available to support math coaches. It is essential to be aware of and access this range of resources if we are all to contribute to the continued evolution of coaching in mathematics. These resources provide multiple opportunities and vehicles through which coaches can come together and engage in ongoing dialogue.

KEYS TO PROFESSIONAL DEVELOPMENT FOR THE COACH

It is critical when establishing coach positions in a district or school to ensure that the coaches have opportunities to develop foundational skills and knowledge, to study practices of coaching, and to reflect in an ongoing manner on their own work. When considering the print and online materials that can serve as resources for the coach's professional development, the following areas of knowledge for the coach will be valuable:

- Interpersonal communication skills
- Content knowledge
- Pedagogical knowledge
- Knowledge of the curriculum
- Practices and strategies of coaching
- Adult learning and development

In addition to reading about these skill sets and knowledge, beginning coaches need opportunities to practice their coaching moves, questioning techniques, and other coaching strategies in a manner that allows them to receive constructive feedback. Cases, such as those used in this book, are a way for coaches to freeze a moment of coaching and examine it for study and learning. These may be cases that the coach writes individually in a journal, or they may be cases that are shared or studied as a group. Establishing forums that bring coaches together as a group, face-to-face or online, allows communities of coaches to grow, communities that can provide coaches with the professional dialogue and support to further develop their work.

Questions for Reflecting and Linking to Practice

1. What are the areas of coaching knowledge or the coaching skill sets that you feel are your strengths? What are those areas that you would like to focus on in the next year?

2. Consider the structures and the range of vehicles for professional development suggested in this chapter—readings, journal writing, coaching simulations, sharing coaching cases with others, and online communities. Which of these are already in place in your school or district for coaches and which need further development?

3. There is the challenge of time that emerges when juggling the work of the coach with the time that needs to be set aside for the coach's professional development. How might a balanced allocation of time be achieved in your school or district?

Conclusion

Coaches are unsung leaders in our schools. They lead with courage. They challenge practices in order to move student learning forward, but they do so with respectful relationships, with a collaborative spirit, and, most important, with a relentless commitment to students and mathematics. This is not always easy.

Coaches lead with humility. They recognize that they are themselves continuing to learn in their own work. They undertake action research to match effective coaching practices to the contexts and cultures of their schools. And yet they recognize that what works today may need to be adapted or revised tomorrow given the context of an ever-changing world that places new demands and constraints on schools.

Coaches are transformational leaders. They seek not only to improve instructional practices and student learning through their coaching work but also to make teachers more reflective. Coaches pose questions to teachers as a tool in their work, but they ultimately move teachers to a point in their professional growth in which they raise questions themselves. This allows a teacher's growth to continue even when the coach is not with him or her. When teachers can raise these questions for themselves, it can create a culture of inquiry and learning in a school, one that is self-sustaining and renewing.

Finally, coaches lead by influence, not by title. This is an important distinction in leadership. The role of influence and the power of interactions is significant (Spillane, 2005). A person can have a formal title of authority and yet not necessarily be perceived by others as being a leader whom they will follow willingly or with commitment. Conversely, a person without a position or title of authority can impact the motivation, beliefs, and behaviors of others; that is, others follow not because they must, but because they desire.

Coaches lead through relationships and connections with teachers. They lead with expertise, passion, and a commitment to student learning. This is powerful leadership. Coaching matters.

Now revisit the opening question of this book: *What is coaching?* What are three new insights into coaching that you have developed from reading this book? What are two questions about coaching that you still have? What is one next step you are going to take to move your own coaching work forward?

Resource A

Resources to Develop Mathematical and Pedagogical Content Knowledge

Developing Mathematical Ideas
(http://www2.edc.org/CDT/DMI/dmicur.html)

Developing Mathematical Ideas (DMI) is a professional development curriculum that is intended to facilitate teachers' thinking through the big ideas of K–7 mathematics and develop a lens for examining how children develop these ideas over time. This is done through a set of case episodes (authored by classroom teachers) that demonstrate student thinking; a facilitator supports a group of teachers in examining the actual mathematics involved in the lesson and unpacking the case through a set of focus questions. Each DMI module presents a coherent set of cases across K–7 grades, providing teachers with opportunities to develop understandings of how mathematical ideas develop for children across the years. Seven DMI seminars are available, addressing number and operations; geometry and measurement; data; and patterns, functions, and change.

Young Mathematicians at Work series
(http://books.heinemann.com)

The Young Mathematicians at Work series was developed under the support of the National Science Foundation by Catherine Towney Fosnot and Maarten Dolk. It provides a series of books and related CD-ROMs that provide a coherent "landscape" of mathematics that young children develop across the elementary school years. There is a focus on the big ideas, strategies, and representations and models that children use to "mathematize" the world. Emphasis is on how the teacher's deep understanding of the mathematical landscape can allow problems to be crafted that bring these big ideas to the forefront for children's thinking and inquiry.

Dynamic Classroom Assessment (http://www.etacuisenaire.com/professionaldevelopment/math/dca/dynamic.jsp)

The Dynamic Classroom Assessment professional development course focuses on developing teachers' ability to authentically assess students' mathematical understandings and to use this knowledge to inform instructional decisions. Emphasis is on the use of effective probing questions and tasks to uncover potential student misconceptions, providing effective feedback to students, and using these insights to adapt instruction to meet the individual needs of students. While assessment is the vehicle of study, the growth for teachers in the course comes from better understanding what students know and are able to do with regard to a given mathematical idea.

First Steps in Mathematics (http://www.stepspd.com)

The First Steps in Mathematics professional development courses and resources are designed to expand teachers' understanding of mathematics and how young children learn math. The development of professional judgment on the part of the teacher is key, and this includes addressing teachers' understanding of mathematical ideas, the instructional experiences that may be implemented, and the understandings and potential misconceptions that children may bring to these experiences. Through the use of student work on diagnostic tasks in the program, teachers map students' level of understanding and are able to focus in on specific key understandings in mathematics that a child may need to develop. The specificity with which teachers are able to discuss a child's mathematics learning—in contrast to broad, vague statements of ability—is a valuable outcome of this training and use of resources for teachers.

Resource B

Sources of Math Coach Professional Development

PRINT RESOURCES: BOOKS

Professional books offer mathematics coaches texts that can be studied independently or as part of a facilitated group of coaches developing their practice collaboratively. Some print resources are specific to mathematics coaching, and their direct link to the work of the elementary mathematics coach is obvious; however, other instructional coaching resources can also provide useful insights into overarching coaching principles and tools that cut across disciplines.

Examples:

Knight, J. (2007). *Instructional coaching: A partnership approach to improving instruction*. Thousand Oaks, CA: Corwin.

Morse, A. (2009). *Cultivating a math coaching practice: A guide for K–8 math educators*. Thousand Oaks, CA: Corwin.

West, L., & Staub, F. (2003). *Content-focused coaching: Transforming mathematics lessons*. Portsmouth, NH: Heinemann.

PRINT RESOURCES: JOURNAL ARTICLES AND SERIES

Journal articles can provide either a broad sweep overview to launch exploration of coaching or present a targeted discussion of one dimension of coaching. They can serve as quick references or reminders for coaches in the field, refocusing work in a timely manner, and they can also serve as springboards for text-based discussions at weekly or monthly coach team meetings. Some professional organizers publish newsletters and series (in print and online) that address teacher leadership and professional development topics and often these include useful coaching articles as well.

Examples:

Feger, S., Woleck, K., & Hickman, P. (2004). How to develop a coaching eye. *Journal of Staff Development*, 25(2), 14–18.

Teachers Teaching Teachers (T3) is a monthly online newsletter of the National Staff Development Council; each issue includes articles that examine teacher-leader challenges and strategies. (http://www.nsdc.org/news/t3/index.cfm)

TRAINING SEMINARS, CONFERENCES, AND INSTITUTES

As the field of mathematics coaching grows, organizations are emerging to provide districts and schools with support in developing a cadre of well-trained coaches. These organizations offer a wide range of job-embedded opportunities for coach support, including workshops, consultant site visits, and intensive weeklong institutes during the summer for coaches or teams of coaches from a district.

Examples:

Mathematics Leadership Program, includes the Center for the Development of Coaching and Math Leadership (http://www.mathleadership.org).

The Professional Development for Math Coaching Institute (PDMC), part of the series of Summer Institutes at Mount Holyoke College. Contact Amy Morse, project director, at amorse@edc.org.

ONLINE LEARNING

Online seminars and courses provide coaches with opportunities not only to have access to coaching resources and tools from a skilled and knowledgeable facilitator, but also to engage in dialogue and become connected with others undertaking the work of the coach. Online coaching networks can bring together groups of people from far-reaching geographic locations who would otherwise be pursuing their coaching work in isolation.

Example:

The Coaching Cycle is an interactive online course for K–8 mathematics coaches. Contact Loretta Heuer at lheuer@edc.org. (http://www2.edc.org/MLT/conference07/k8/default.html)

References

Center for Cognitive Coaching. (2009). *Overview of cognitive coaching.* Retrieved September 14, 2007, from http://www.cognitivecoaching.com/overview.

Collins, J. (2001). *Good to great: Why some companies make the leap . . . and others don't.* New York: HarperCollins.

Feger, S., & Woleck, K. (2007, April). *Supporting mathematics coaching through development and research of online seminars.* Paper presented at NSF Teacher Professional Continuum Conference on Instructional Coaching in Mathematics: Researchers and Practitioners Learning From Each Other, Boston, MA.

Feger, S., Woleck, K., & Hickman, P. (2004). How to develop a coaching eye. *Journal of Staff Development, 25*(2), 14–18.

Fosnot, C. T., Dolk, M., & Cameron, A. (2001). *Young mathematicians at work: Constructing number sense, addition, and subtraction.* Portsmouth, NH: Heinemann.

Hord, S., Rutherford, W., Huling-Austin, L., & Hall, G. (1987). *Taking charge of change.* Alexandria, VA: Association for Supervision and Curriculum Development.

Kliman, M., Tierney, C., Russell, S. J., Murray, M., & Akers, J. (2004). *Mathematical thinking at Grade 5: Introduction and landmarks in the number system.* (Investigations in Number, Data, and Space series). Glenview, IL: Pearson Scott Foresman.

Knight, J. (2004). *What instructional coaches do.* Retrieved August 21, 2008, from http://www.instructionalcoach.org/about.html.

Knight, J. (2006, April). Instructional coaching: Eight factors for realizing better classroom teaching through support, feedback and intensive, individualized professional learning. *The School Administrator.* Retrieved November 18, 2009, http://www.aasa.org/SchoolAdministratorArticle.aspx?id=9584.

Knight, J. (2007). *Instructional coaching: A partnership approach to improving instruction.* Thousand Oaks, CA: Corwin.

Koh, S., & Neuman, S. B. (2006). *Exemplary elements of coaching.* Ann Arbor: University of Michigan Research Program on Ready to Read.

Massachusetts Department of Education. (2007, April). *Characteristics of standards-based mathematics coaching.* Draft.

Silicon Valley Mathematics Initiative (SVMI). (2007a). *Pedagogical content coaching.* Retrieved October 15, 2007, from http://www.noycefdn.org/documents/math/PedagogicalContentCoaching.pdf.

Silicon Valley Mathematics Initiative (SVMI). (2007b). *Philosophy and overview.* Retrieved October 15, 2007, from http://www.noycefdn.org/math/documents/SVMIPhilosophy_Overview.pdf (no longer available).

Sparks, D. (1990). Cognitive coaching: An interview with Robert Garmston. *Journal of Staff Development, 11*(2), 12–15.

Spillane, J. P. (2005). *Distributed leadership.* San Francisco: Jossey-Bass.

Victoria Department of Education, Employment, and Training. (2001). *Early numeracy interview booklet.* Victoria, Australia: Curriculum Press.

West, L., & Staub, F. C. (2003). *Content-focused coaching: Transforming mathematics lessons.* Portsmouth, NH: Heinemann.

Index

CORWIN

A SAGE Company

The Corwin logo—a raven striding across an open book—represents the union of courage and learning. Corwin is committed to improving education for all learners by publishing books and other professional development resources for those serving the field of PreK–12 education. By providing practical, hands-on materials, Corwin continues to carry out the promise of its motto: **"Helping Educators Do Their Work Better."**